EGYPT
and the
HOLY LAND
In Historic Photographs

EGYPT
and the
HOLY LAND
In Historic Photographs

77 Views by
Francis Frith

Introduction & Bibliography by
Julia Van Haaften
Art & Architecture Division, New York Public Library

Selection & Commentary by
Jon E. Manchip White
Lindsay Young Professor of the Humanities and
Professor of English, University of Tennessee, Knoxville

Dover Publications, Inc.
New York

Published in Canada by General Publishing Company, Ltd., 30 Lesmill Road, Don Mills, Toronto, Ontario.
Published in the United Kingdom by Constable and Company, Ltd., 10 Orange Street, London WC2H 7EG.

Egypt and the Holy Land in Historic Photographs: 77 Views by Francis Frith is a new work, first published by Dover Publications, Inc., in 1980. The photographs are a selection from those that originally appeared in the four-volume series published by William Mackenzie, London, ca. 1862, with the titles (I) *Sinai and Palestine;* (II) *Lower Egypt, Thebes, and the Pyramids;* (III) *Upper Egypt and Ethiopia;* (IV) *Egypt, Sinai, and Palestine. Supplementary Volume.*

Book design by Carol Belanger Grafton

International Standard Book Number: 0-486-24048-7
Library of Congress Catalog Card Number: 80-66612

Manufactured in the United States of America
Dover Publications, Inc.
180 Varick Street
New York, N.Y. 10014

ACKNOWLEDGMENTS

In the course of my research on Francis Frith's photographic expeditions in the Middle East it was my good fortune to have had the vast and knowledgeably staffed collections of the Research Libraries of The New York Public Library at my disposal. These divisions deserve special thanks: Art & Architecture, Cooperative Services, General Research & Humanities, Rare Books, Oriental, and Science & Technology. Other helpful libraries were the Epstean Collection, Columbia University; the Prints & Photographs Division, Library of Congress; and the Graphic Arts Library, Princeton University.

I must also thank these individuals who provided special materials, information and/ or advice: Phoebe Frith Johannes and John Frith, great-grandchildren of Francis Frith, who graciously read the manuscript; William Culp Darrah; Philippe Garner; Arthur T. Gill, Royal Photographic Society; Martha E. Jenks and Andrew Eskind, International Museum of Photography/George Eastman House; Janet Lehr; James Reilly, Rochester Institute of Technology; Eliot Wald; Richard F. Willers; and Laurence Wood, British Library. Of course, my use of what was provided and the results are entirely my own responsibility. My final thanks must go to my husband Ron Schick for his welcome comments, his help with photographic logistics and his unflagging enthusiasm for my work.

J.V.H.

CONTENTS

INTRODUCTION
by Julia Van Haaften

Salaam!—Peace be with thee, oh, thou pleasant buyer of my book. It is my intention, should my life be spared, and should the present undertaking prove successful, to present to the public, from time to time, my impressions of foreign lands, illustrated by photographic views![1]

So Francis Frith first introduced himself in 1858 in the beginning of his inaugural book *Egypt and Palestine Photographed and Described.* His expressed hopes were actually fulfilled for his life was long—76 years—and his publications wildly successful. Having made his fortune when he was just 34, Frith set off for Egypt in 1856 completely equipped for photography in that desert land. The photographic views and sterographs that he brought back from this and two subsequent journeys to the Middle East* immediately established his reputation as a leading photographer of the day. With *Egypt and Palestine* as his initial effort, Frith also established himself as the first entrepreneur-photographer promoting the large-scale production of first-rate scenic and architectural photographs of exotic lands.

Helmut Gernsheim, the photographic historian, has noted:

Frith's fame nowadays rests chiefly on the many publications which ensued from his three tours to Egypt, Nubia, Palestine, and Syria, for these exemplify his finest—and at the same time earliest—work . . . .[2]

Frith's books of views combined a light yet informative narrative with astoundingly realistic and evocative images of all the major monuments of the ancient Middle East. In the best tradition of armchair travel, the photographic volumes were intended to entertain and inform their audience. An educated man and a printer by profession, Frith understood the value and appeal of such handsomely illustrated books. All the photo-view books Frith published (see the Bibliography following this Introduction) have, with the exception of the Bibles, the same basic format: each albumen print has been trimmed and pasted onto a letterpress mount and is accompanied by one or two pages of descriptive text.

Interweaving his narrative with archaeological and ethnographic details, Frith wrote of personal experiences with the local populations, his encounters with wild animals and, most fascinating, his photographic manipulations under adverse field conditions. Even the two volumes of Frith's views with text by the mother and son Egyptologists Mrs. Sophia Poole and Reginald Stuart Poole contain personal recollection and

opinion in addition to archaeology. Charmingly written, handsome and exotic, Frith's publications were some of the ultimate drawing-room-table books of their day.

Frith also recognized the religious and historical fascination that the names Egypt and Palestine† held for the Victorian public. His first trip lasted from September 1856 to July 1857; Frith reached the colossal figures at Abu Simbel below the Second Cataract of the Nile, the southernmost goal of most tourists in Egypt and Nubia at the time. During a four-month return to England, Frith negotiated contracts to publish stereographs and larger views from his negatives and then was off again from November 1857 to May 1858, traveling via Egypt by boat to Jaffa in order to reach Jerusalem, Syria and Lebanon. During his second return to England, which lasted over a year, he witnessed the success of *Egypt and Palestine,* launched with publisher James S. Virtue in London and New York. Frith's third and final Middle Eastern trip began in the summer of 1859 and lasted well into the next year. He revisited Cairo and the Nile, pushing further south than any previous photographer, to Soleb in Egyptian-ruled Nubia, well beyond the Second Cataract at Wadi Halfa. Frith concluded this last expedition to the East by crossing the Sinai via the southern route and rephotographing sites as far north as Jerusalem.

By 1860, with the completion of his third expedition, Frith was the owner of a thriving photographic-view concern, the largest in England. F. Frith & Co., Reigate, continued in business until its liquidation in 1971,[3] and is now managed as a picture research collection.[4] Today we value Frith's Middle Eastern photographs both for the pioneering role they have played in expeditionary topographical photography and for their exquisite documentary ability to hold intact a world now radically altered by archaeology, tourism and political evolution.

FRANCIS FRITH

Francis Frith was born in 1822 in Chesterfield, Derbyshire, to Quaker parents.[5] Solid middle-class citizens without artistic inclinations, the Friths sent the adolescent Francis to the Camp Hill Quaker boarding school in Birmingham for four years. Though he was excited by the study of humanistic and

---

* [In the captions to the plates, by Professor White, "Near East" refers, of course, to the same region.—PUBLISHER]

† [Throughout this book "Palestine" is used in its ancient geographical sense, with no reference to its special meaning in contemporary politics.—PUBLISHER]

scientific disciplines, the experience left him with an intense contempt for the routine of school life: "If I have a nightmare, I dream of going back to school," he wrote years later in his unpublished autobiography. At 16, he left school—"the most insipid and mechanical portion of existence"—for good. This is not to say that Frith despised learning: papers and published works throughout his long life reveal an enduring interest in metaphysics, poetry, engineering and, of course, travel and history. Though in his first book, *Egypt and Palestine*, he modestly deprecated his ability as a writer—"I dare not revise—out goes one half that I have written, and the remainder is intolerably dull"—those same words reveal an understanding of the attraction his own very charming exuberance would have for his readers.

Free of school, Francis was apprenticed by his parents to a Sheffield cutlery firm from which, like school, he felt he derived nothing of value. His apprenticeship ended after five years with what would, in all likelihood, be recognized today as a nervous breakdown. Frith spent the next few years traveling in England, Wales and Scotland, resting and recovering. Not without some means, he was able to enter a successful grocery partnership in Liverpool. In 1850, when he was 28, he dissolved the partnership and established his own independent printing business in the same city. That business thrived and early in 1856 Frith was able to realize a substantial profit by selling the firm to his major competitor. At 34, he had become a man of independent means.

The origin of Frith's initial photographic activity is unknown. It is temptingly romantic—though completely undocumentable—to speculate that Frith, on his recuperative travels through Scotland in the 1840s, could have observed and been inspired by the famous W. H. Fox Talbot while that pioneer was making calotypes for his 1845 book *Sun-Pictures in Scotland.* In any event, with the patent-free invention of the wet-collodion-on-glass process by Frederick Scott Archer in 1851, practical photography became accessible to all who would learn its procedures. In March 1853 Frith was one of only three (out of seven total) founders of the Liverpool Photographic Society enrolled with the membership status of "professional" at the group's first official meeting.[6]

Many advances and high points in the history of photography have been due to the close alliance between the photographer's and the printer's crafts. After all, the impetus to the discovery of photography was Niépce's search for a method to render permanent the image produced by a camera obscura or camera lucida so that he could make a printing plate from it. Niépce (and his more successful followers) believed that a method using light to transfer images for printing in ink would be an accurate, cheaper and more productive way of publishing large numbers of pictures—both from the hands of artists and "from nature"—for which there was a ready market. The photomechanical processes of today (not to mention all the intervening and obsolete ones) are direct descendants of the intentions and discoveries of Niépce, Daguerre and Talbot, the fathers of photography.

It requires no great leap of imagination to understand how photography, with its truthful impact and scientific realism, might appeal to a young modern Victorian printer and businessman like Francis Frith. The first English photo publisher (following the modest productions of W. H. Fox Talbot in the 1840s and the more prolific Blanquart-Évrard in France) to meet the Victorian public's demand for topographical photo views, Frith can rightly be considered the first mass-producer and distributor of photographic images in England. With a voluminous output of foreign and local views, his post-Middle East firm, F. Frith & Co., Reigate, processed and sold millions of photos for framing, album mounting, postcards, stereographs and book illustrations well into the period of successful halftone printing. In sum, Frith's story is important not only for his remarkable photographs of the Middle East but also for his significance as a benchmark in the larger history of publishing and visual communication.

Although Frith helped found the Liverpool Photographic Society in 1853, he seems to have held no office in it nor contributed enough at subsequent meetings to be mentioned in their reported minutes. His original status as a "professional" member may have been overly optimistic or just premature, for early in 1856 his photographs on view in London at the Photographic Society's exhibition were praised this way by a hometown reviewer: "The best portraits are those by our member, Mr. Frith, an amateur."[7]

No matter what his status, Frith was making photographs during the hazy period before his Middle Eastern excursions brought him such fame. There are some undated, but signed-in-the-negative, stereo views of the British countryside on hand-lettered lavender mounts; to judge by their "homemade" quality, they probably predate Frith's professional work and his first Egyptian excursion.[8] It has also been suggested that Frith's pre-Egypt views of Cambridge were used by author Charles Henry Cooper to illustrate his 1860 edition of Thomas Wright's *Memorials of Cambridge.*[9] At home, Frith must have been very active as an amateur photo manipulator for he revealed that his mother, in consternation at having to launder his silver-salt-stained shirts, chided him for his work in "the Black Art," a common early epithet for photography.[10]

However, the most interesting evidence of Frith's pre-Egypt photography are the five extant mammoth-plate (16-by-20-inch) collodion-on-glass negatives signed "Frith 1856" that are now in New York collector Janet Lehr's possession. Three of the plates depict local cathedral ruins and two record railroad bridges. One of the bridges is Robert Stephenson's 1850 Britannia Bridge over the Menai Straits. Constructed in Egyptian Revival style, it may have served as a witty visual prelude to the sights Frith anticipated photographing later that year in Egypt.

Egypt and the Holy Land

Frith introduced his first publication of photo views with this claim: "I have chosen as a beginning of my labours, the two most interesting lands of the globe—EGYPT and PALESTINE."[11] The choice of locale for his first photographic venture is partly a reflection of his genuine religious feeling and strong desire to experience those significant locations at first hand. Also, Egypt was then a topic of currency in Europe because of the 1856 pact between Egypt and Ferdinand de Lesseps granting a concession for the construction of the Suez Canal. Although the effect was not immediate, the pact caused British and foreign officials to shift their Middle East focus from Constantinople to Cairo.

Concurrently, after centuries of wanton treasure hunting, archaeology was finally on the threshold of legitimacy as a scholarly pursuit. Also, in painting and the decorative arts, Middle Eastern subjects had been popular with artists even before the Napoleonic conquest of Egypt. For the Victorians, the exotic and sensual orientalism of the scenery and the semi-clad figures permitted safe relief from the overriding repression of the age.

Throughout the nineteenth century, both Egypt and the Holy Land became increasingly frequent—though still exotic—destinations for travelers on the "Grand Tour." Two extremely popular books of the 1840s set the tone for such travel, either in person or via the parlor armchair. The first was *Eōthen,* by Alexander William Kinglake, which appeared anonymously in 1844 and recounted in a spirited and personal manner the author's 1835 excursion overland from Greece to Egypt.[12] The lively character of the narrator, quite the opposite of the real-life Kinglake, made *Eōthen* an immediate sensation; in one edition or another, it has remained in print nearly to the present day. The second popular travel book was also a personal account. Under the pseudonym Titmarsh, William Makepeace Thackeray published his version of a similar tour: *Notes of a Journey from Cornhill to Grand Cairo* (1846). Though not as widely reissued as *Eōthen,* its confiding tone and the author's identity made it famous.

However, the intimacy which the early Victorians felt with these exotic and historic lands was mocked by the lack of accurate visual information. Artists had drawn the monuments, of course, and there had been some photographic activity, but in 1856, the year Frith first set out for the East, Egypt, the Nile and the Holy Land were still geographies of considerable mystery.

Up to this date the most complete visual record of the area had been the six-volume collection of colored lithographs by Louis Haghe after drawings made in the 1830s by the Scottish painter and Royal Academician, David Roberts. Published between 1842 and 1849 with texts by scholars George Croly and William Brockedon, the series was extraordinarily successful. Demand for it was incessant and *The Holy Land, Syria, Idumea, Arabia, Egypt & Nubia from Drawings Made on the Spot by David Roberts* was reissued in 1855–1856. It is not impossible that the success of Roberts' work prompted Frith, who recognized the superiority of photo images, to turn his photographic publishing ambition to the East.

It is also important to remember that expeditions to the source of the Nile and to central Africa were still in the future. Frith embarked two years before Sir Richard Burton and John Speke set out to discover the source of the Nile, while the successful Livingstone-Stanley quest was more than a decade away. However, Egypt and the Middle East were changing rapidly. The reign of Western-educated Said Pasha in the 1850s saw the adoption of European customs, social behavior and dress by the Egyptian court and upper class. The old ways were losing ground to those of the economically dominant European business community. Frith lived in the first age of rapidly changing technology; surely, his sense of history and the threat to vanishing monuments and relics were also among his major motivations:

> I may be allowed to state, as giving additional value to good Photographs of eastern antiquities, that a change is rapidly passing over many of the most interesting: in addition to the corroding tooth of Time and the ceaseless drifting of the remorseless sand, Temples and Tombs are exposed to continued plundering—Governors of districts take the huge blocks of stone, and the villagers walk off with the available bricks, whilst travellers of all nations break up and carry off, without scruple, the most interesting of the sculptured friezes and the most beautiful of the architectural ornaments.[13]

Therefore, Frith's choice of Egypt and the Holy Land was the result of several personal factors plus his astute awareness of the existence of a like-minded Victorian public as a ready market for his photographs. Indeed, Frith rode the crest of a wave of public interest in topographical photography. Noting that such was already the case in England, a correspondent from the United States admonished his fellow photographers early in 1856:

> There would be a great demand for landscapes if any were offered for sale, because in the importing stores a very large number of actinic pictures [photographs] are sold, not only of the celebrated localities and buildings, . . . but of numerous unknown scenes, even without the intimation of locality beyond the beauty of the picture itself.[14]

The texts of all Frith's Egypt and Holy Land publications center largely on the archaeology and ethnography of the areas, though his personal adventures and opinions are frequently and charmingly recorded. However, it is an interesting gauge of Frith's personal reserve that questionings of faith or theology are almost completely absent from his commentaries. The most telling remark he made about the historical existence of Biblical sites is this: "I imagine that the contemporaries of these great events would be much more likely than future generations to overlook, and even disregard, the precise localities of their occurrence, being absorbed and satisfied by the events themselves."[15] Frith was not unfamiliar with contemporary scholarship in Egyptian and Palestine studies. He quoted from favorite authorities when he felt it useful, though he was a sensible, clearsighted man who recognized jargon when he read it. He even quoted it for his readers' pleasure; here, from a "popular" article on Baalbek: "The building is peripteral, the columns are pycnostyle, and the portico is dipteral, with a pseudo-intercolumniation before the antae of the pronaos!"[16]

For Egyptian background, Frith most frequently referred to Sir John Gardner Wilkinson, whose *Architecture of Ancient Egypt* (1850) was probably his main source of information. Wilkinson's researches had also been published in 1847 as *Murray's Handbook for Travellers in Egypt; . . . the Nile, . . . the Peninsula of Mt. Sinai,* which Frith may have used on his third journey, since a revised edition appeared in 1858. Frith also mentioned Dr. Heinrich Karl Brugsch, whose *Reiseberichte aus Aegypten* appeared in 1855. Brugsch, like Frith, was traveling in Egypt in 1857–58; it would seem, from the manner in which Frith quoted Brugsch's views, that the two young men may have met and exchanged opinions and, perhaps, photographs.

Palestine, more remote than Egypt for the European tourist, was covered in Edward Robinson's *Biblical Researches in Palestine and the Adjacent Regions* (1856). Fully recounting everyday dealings with sheiks, shepherds, guides and others, Robinson's narrative, in addition to identifying localities and correcting numerous geographical questions, prepared Frith in depth for his encounter with the Holy Land. Frith also consulted Arthur Penrhyn Stanley's *Sinai and Palestine* (1856, 1862), quoting from it in one of his later publications, and revealing a skeptic's disregard for pedantry:

> As there are modes of swindling in commerce which are *almost* respectable, and which by no means subject the peculiar class of tradesmen who practise them to the penalties of the law—so, in book-making, a kind of pilferage is largely and systematically practised, which is very nearly creditable, inasmuch as it injures no one very much, and, if cleverly disguised, is called "research," and redounds to the credit of the thief. To ensure admiration, one needs only to acknowledge that the article is pilfered, and from whom. This I confess, without professing anything.[17]

Archaeology never repaid Frith the compliment. Despite his considerable documentary contributions, mention of his name and his original, widely published work is inexplicably absent from standard histories of Egyptian and Middle East archaeology.[18] This is especially curious, since Frith's three expeditions in the late 1850s coincide with the beginnings of serious, systematic research in these regions. Although the Napoleonic conquest of Egypt at the turn of the century prompted a period of disorganized excavations, generally carried out by diplomats and adventurers, those expeditions served largely to capture monuments and art works that soon found their way into national museums and private collections. Giovanni Battista Belzoni, the most famous adventurer, and Jean-François Champollion, the first Egyptologist, both date from this wanton period. The same situation existed on a smaller scale in Palestine and Mesopotamia.

Frith expressed his uncomprehending contempt for both the pillaged and the pillagers, having seen it all at first hand. His outburst is a solid expression of our contemporary concept of "national treasures" and at the same time is extraordinarily self-righteous:

> What can we think of a government which has systematically authorized travellers of all nations to mutilate or carry off its proudest specimens of ancient art?—an irreparable injury, which can indicate only the most barbarous carelessness of these unique treasures. Hundreds of these beautiful sculptures now enrich the museums and private collections of all Europe, but only the intelligent Egyptian traveller can fully appreciate their loss *to Egypt*. Methinks it were better that a *few* men who will be at the pains of seeking them in their legitimate places should enjoy them as they can only *there* be enjoyed, rather than that the hordes of careless people who throng the British Museum even should smile thoughtlessly at their incongruous quaintness, and, in England, their unintelligible grandeur.[19]

In 1850 the French appointed a Directeur des Services des Antiquités in Egypt, and a period marked by more conscientious discovery and investigation began. In the rest of the Middle East, equivalent systematic work was not underway until the 1860s.

When Frith set out on his first journey in 1856, popular knowledge of the region's pre-Christian history was tied exclusively to Biblical tradition. Religious faith and pilgrimage remained the strongest lures for travelers to the Holy Land. Francis Frith integrated his entrepreneurial sensibility with a sincere religious faith. He recognized that as documents of religious and geographic interest and as evidence of the new science of archaeology, his views would have wide appeal.

Though Francis Frith is the most prominent of the early photographers of Egypt and the Holy Land, he was by no means the first.[20] The land of Egypt was linked immediately with photography in Dominique-François Arago's 1839 public statement of Daguerre's process, which claimed as one of the new invention's benefits its ability, invaluable to archaeology, to accurately and quickly record hieroglyphic inscriptions.[21] Exotic and so very ancient, Egypt outranked such other antique sites as Rome and Athens for early photographers' attention. Painter Horace Vernet went to Egypt late in 1839 with his nephew, bringing back daguerreotypes, now lost, that were published as engravings in the series *Les Excursions daguerriennes*. Others daguerreotyped as well, to have their work copied by graphic artists onto aquatint plates for conventional printing. Joly de Lotbinière's daguerreotypy for Hector Horeau's *Panorama d'Égypte et de Nubie* (1841) is a well-known example.[22] Rediscovered in 1952, daguerreotypist Joseph-Philibert Girault de Prangey is known to have traveled in the Middle East in 1842–1845. Many of the plates in his *Monuments arabes d'Égypte, de Syrie, et d'Asie mineure* (1846) are drawn after daguerreotypes.[23]

Writers followed, with cameras in hand. The early romantic Gérard de Nerval failed completely in 1843 with his daguerreotype outfit. The young friends Gustave Flaubert and Maxime DuCamp were much more successful in 1849–1851 working with paper negatives.[24] DuCamp, who went on to become a popular and prolific travel writer and journalist, brought back at least 120 usable negatives of monuments in Egypt and the Holy Land. The photographs were published with his commentary in 1852: *Égypte, Nubie, Palestine et Syrie* was printed by Blanquart-Évrard in an edition of unknown size. The soft, true-black salt prints, gold-toned for permanence, measured about 225 by 160 mm.[25]

In addition to the early daguerreotypists and the well-known DuCamp, there were other photographers of lesser significance in Egypt in the 1850s whose works are now being rediscovered. J. B. Greene, a member of the Société Asiatique, published *Le Nil* in 1854.[26] Robert Murray, chief engineer to the Viceroy of Egypt, showed Egyptian photographs, to great praise, in 1858.[27] Also in 1858 Félix Teynard produced *L'Égypte et Nubie*, containing photographs made in 1851.[28] Frank Haes reportedly made transparent stereos of Cairo before 1858.[29] The Englishman Felice Beato and his brother-in-law James Robertson photographed in Cairo and vicinity in 1858–1860 and showed their work in London.[30] Francis Bedford accompanied the Prince of Wales on a goodwill tour through Egypt and the Holy Land in 1862; his 172 12-by-10-inch views were received with lavish praise when exhibited and later published.[31] The July 15, 1862 issue of *The Photographic Journal*, which announced the photography prizewinners at the 1862 International Exhibition, cited three photographers in addition to Frith for their views of Middle Eastern subjects.[32] By 1865 photography had made Egyptian monuments so familiar that a popular essayist could describe the colossi between Luxor and the Ramasseum as "well known to fame and photographists."[33] In subsequent years such photographers as Félix Bonfils, Antonio Beato and Pascal Sébah were the dominant suppliers of souvenir photographs for the sophisticated tourist trade.

In general, photographic activity began much more slowly in Palestine, although there is one early exception. Traveling with his father, the Rev. Dr. Alexander Keith, in 1844, Dr. George Skene Keith of Scotland took 30 daguerreotypes in Palestine and Syria, as well as some views in Petra. Eighteen of these daguerreotypes were published as engravings in the thirty-sixth edition of his father's *Evidence of the Truth of the Christian Religion* (1848).[34] DuCamp had been in the area by 1850–1851 and his views were included in the 1852 volume mentioned previously. In 1854, Auguste Salzmann photographed Jerusalem using the calotype process. With photographs printed, like DuCamp's, by Blanquart-Évrard, Salzmann's *Jerusalem* appeared in 1856 with 40 calotypes of scenery and monuments. Frith, in 1858, was the next to photograph here. In 1859–1860, John Cramb of Glasgow toured the Holy Land. His views were published as *Jerusalem in 1860* with letterpress by the Rev. Robert Buchanan.[35] Francis Bedford's 1862 tour with the Prince of Wales as far north as Syria and Lebanon has already been discussed. Gustave Le Gray (who had been DuCamp's teacher) finally made the trip in 1860. Although his leg was broken when he was kicked by a packhorse in Syria, he was able to continue photographing.[36] These individual photographers were followed in the early 1860s by the Ordnance Survey under Captain Charles W. Wilson. *Ordnance Survey of Jerusalem*, a textless volume of 76 albumen prints by Sergeant J. MacDonald and commercial photographer P. Bergheim, including some multiprint panoramas, appeared in 1865. That same year the London-based Palestine Exploration Fund was founded; it sponsored extensive photo documentation of the area.[37]

There is no evidence that Francis Frith even knew of such large early projects as those of DuCamp and Salzmann, much less that he felt they or others on a smaller scale represented any competition to his planned publications. Rather, Frith's probable goal was to rival the mammoth production of lithographs after David Roberts' drawings which dominated the mid-Victorian conception of Egypt and the Holy Land.

Photographic Techniques

Frith stands out from other Middle Eastern photographers as the only one to approach his subjects systematically.[38] Frith photographed most monuments at least twice on each visit, usually in a long shot or overview and then in a detail or from a close, revealing angle; for example, Philae, Thebes, Karnak, the Pyramids and Jerusalem are all repeated. Sometimes the photo pair consists of a vertical close-up (especially in Egypt to show how the ruins loom up out of the desert) and a suitably horizontal distant view to take in the surrounding vista. "The Statues of Memnon, Plain of Thebes" are typical of Frith's selection of two comparative vantage points. He also photographed some monuments from different perspectives but at roughly equal distances so that viewers could reconstruct some of the spatial relationships between the remaining elements of the ruined architecture. His many Cairo and Jerusalem cityscapes accomplish the same goal. Nearly all of Frith's photographs—but especially the Egyptian ones, where geometry is dominant—exploit the delineating shadows cast by a raking morning sun to reveal the form and surface ornament of the surviving monuments. Human figures abound in the photographs from all three trips but their intention and placement changed somewhat. The earliest views contain figures—both European and local—whose nearby lounging presence provides the scale Frith apparently sought. In the later views there are no Europeans; the figures that do appear serve as picturesque counterpoints and small details in the overall compositions.

Unlike his predecessors, Frith carefully coded and numbered his negatives as he made them. The glass plates are signed and the earlier ones (1857 and 1858) are frequently dated. These inscriptions—achieved by scratching in mirror writing into the developed negative emulsion—can be seen on the lower edges of many of the reproductions in this volume. The consecutive numbering on these negatives provides a neat record of Frith's itinerary and gauges the size of his successful photographic output.

On all three trips Frith took stereographs, whole-plate photos (8 by 10 inches) and large-format views (16 by 20 inches) by the wet collodion-on-glass process. His oft-quoted remarks about working in a hot, dry climate are valuable to us for restoring a healthy regard for the consistently high quality achieved by Frith and his fellow explorer-photographers under the most adverse and daunting of conditions:

> The difficulties which I had to overcome in working collodion, in those hot and dry climates, were also very serious. When (at the Second Cataract, one thousand miles from the mouth of the Nile, with the thermometer at 110° in my tent) the collodion actually boiled when poured upon the glass plate, I almost despaired of success.[39]

While no inventory of Frith's equipment survives, the following contemporary list may give an idea of the apparatus necessary for warm-weather expeditionary photography:

1. 10 × 8 inch camera [Frith also had a 20-by-16-inch outfit]
2. stereoscopic camera
3. Smartt's dark tent [and—as Frith related in some detail—tombs, caves, etc. as were handy for excluding light]
4. India rubber cushions in boxes for glass plates
5. bath of glass in cork inclosures as insulation against heat and to absorb shock
6. chemicals in cork lined boxes[40]

Frith had at least two special pieces of equipment made for his first trip: a special shutter in May 1856 with a flap arrangement for a landscape lens by the pioneering lensmaker Andrew Ross,[41] and a darkroom wagon:

> Know, then, that for the purpose of making large pictures (20 inches by 16), I had constructed in London a wicker-work carriage on wheels, which was, in fact, both camera and developing room, and occasionally *sleeping room; . . . .* This carriage of mine, then, being entirely overspread with a loose cover of white sailcloth to protect it from the sun, was a most conspicuous and mysterious-looking vehicle, and excited amongst the Egyptian populace a vast amount of ingenious speculation as to its uses. The idea, however, which seemed the most reasonable, and therefore obtained the most, was that therein, with right laudable and jealous care, I transported from place to place—my—harem! It was full of moon-faced beauties, my wives all!—and great was the respect and consideration which this view of the case procured for me![42]

While Frith has left no further verbal details of his equipment, he allowed his camera, apparently by oversight, to include further illuminating evidence within his careful compositions. For example, his picturesque view "Valley of the Tombs of the Kings, Thebes" shows three laden donkeys, which may well be his own pack animals bearing his burdensome photographic apparatus.[43] Frith's wickerwork carriage peeks out from a ravine in a view of Cairo from the third trip.[44] It is a squarish vehicle with high, spoked wheels and, as Frith described, a white fabric cover. Frith must have had to trundle the contraption far into the desert in search of proper views in its none-too-wide-angle lens, for his wagon's tracks appear in the foreground desert sand of at least one mammoth view.[45] A good illustration of his 8-by-10-inch view camera and tripod appears in the far left of a large, 15-by-19-inch, view of the much photographed temple at Karnak published in the Pooles' *Egypt, Sinai, and Jerusalem.*[46] The Nile boat, or *dahibieh,* on which Frith traveled as far as Abu Simbel on the first trip appears in a pair of photos of the same scene at Philae made with two different cameras—the 8-by-10-inch and the 16-by-20-inch—and are interesting for the variations produced by the change in scale.[47] The large view also shows Frith's little photographic boat with its darkroom tent deployed for use.

The wet-collodion process was still new when Frith set out in 1856. While the process was the most reliable and sharpest negative system in existence, it was exceedingly cumbersome: a glass plate was flooded with the collodion solution, which adhered to the glass as a film; the filmed glass was then "excited" by immersion in a silver-salt solution and was ready for placement in the camera for exposure for whatever length of time would produce a good range of tones—in Frith's case, six to 45 seconds. Processing or development took place soon afterward, out of the direct sun, as did fixing, washing and drying. No prints were made in the field, as inspection of the developed negative was sufficient to insure that a proper exposure had been made. Years later, Frith's friend, the photographic chemist T. Frederick Hardwich, recalled Frith's accomplished technique for handling the large-format wet plates at his Reigate establishment:

His plates were so large that when I first saw him developing a negative it looked to me like a man balancing the top of a small table on his fingers and pouring a jug of water over it. I was curious to see whether he would ever get the developer back again into the vessel without spilling; but this feat he accomplished with much dexterity.[48]

Both *The Photographic Journal* and *The British Journal of Photography* contain complaints and bits of advice from photographers working in British colonies with distinctly un-British climates. The worst problems occurred in the humid tropics: India, the Caribbean and so on. Insect infestation in camera cabinets, collapse of expert joinery and chemical deterioration were recurrent themes. Frith fared a little better, having only heat and dust to combat. This final step from a procedures list for a hot-climate process provides an interesting clue to the laissez-faire techniques used by photographers at home and in the field before photographic chemistry was more fully understood: "Wash with distilled water. Fix with hyposulfite solution, usual strength. Then thoroughly wash *until the water is tasteless*" [italics mine].[49]

Knowing that he could not repeat a several-thousand-mile journey to redo a poor photograph, the expeditionary photographer was under some pressure to have his work proceed normally and to achieve photographic permanence.[50] Variations were cause for concern. Frith seems not to have bothered with distilled water (quite a luxury, really) at the Sea of Galilee: "I detected, by the difficulty which I found in using the water of the lake for photographic purposes, that it is impregnated with a considerable quantity of saline matter."[51] The two photographs Frith published of this area seem not to have suffered greatly, and in fact appear to have a wider tonal range than other Palestine views about which he made no technical complaints.

THE EXPEDITIONS AND THE PHOTOGRAPHS

My labours, as regards this publication, are now at an end. I regret many imperfections, of which I am fully conscious. I regret, especially, that I was so grievously hurried whilst taking my views: most undoubtedly I might have done more justice to my subjects—yet, when I reflect upon the circumstances under which many of the Photographs were taken, I marvel greatly that they turned out so well. Now in a smothering little tent, with my collodion fizzing—boiling up all over the glass the instant that it touched—and, again, pushing my way backwards, upon my hands and knees, into a damp, slimy rock-tomb, to manipulate—it is truly marvellous that the results should be presentable at all. Yet I have to thank the public for a most flattering and kind reception, and a most decided "success."[52]

So Frith concludes *Egypt and Palestine Photographed and Described*, the first of his planned publications. A total of 76 photos appeared in 25 subscription parts between January 1858 and early spring 1860, in separate English and American editions. The English price was ten shillings per issue; the American, three dollars. The list of 274 English subscribers issued with the London edition shows about one in 15 to be members of the clergy. The photographs in *Egypt and Palestine* are all from Frith's first two trips; i.e. from 1856–1858. The 9-by-7-inch Egyptian views are numbered with the prefix "E"; those from Palestine begin with "P." The "E" sequence starts with images from Nubia, indicating that Frith traveled south on the Nile to Abu Simbel before beginning to photograph in earnest. The first 70 or so "E" photos are also signed with the date 1857; the "P" series is undated.

Francis Frith first embarked for Egypt from Liverpool in 1856, unnoticed by the photography press of the day. His friend and traveling companion, Francis Herbert Wenham (1824–1908), was making the journey to advise Frith on optics and related photographic matters. An adept mechanical and optical engineer, Wenham was also a founding member of the Royal Aeronautical Society, and is now regarded as one of the principal theoreticians of modern aviation as well as the designer of the biplane. The observations he made of birds along the Nile formed the basis for his famous paper "Aerial Locomotion" published in 1866.[53] The Wright Brothers acknowledged Wenham as "one of the ablest and most useful men who have laboured in the cause of human flight."[54] Wenham invented the small steam-powered yacht which he and Frith used for transportation; upon their return to Cairo the reigning Pasha supposedly purchased the small craft.[55] It is probably Wenham who, wearing a wide-brimmed hat, appears as a picturesque scale indicator in several of the photos from the first Egyptian trip.

Though Frith wrote the following words at least a year after his first trip down the Nile, they communicate the exuberance and freedom he brought to this pioneering photography:

Do not imagine, O my readers, that your artist kept a diary of his feelings; he never *could* get beyond the second page of such a record: and here, at Philae, he had indeed other work. During his stay the rising sun saw him, encumbered with "baths" and bottles, scrambling up the bank from his dahibieh, by the base of this "Bed of Pharaoh;" and as the declining rays gilded its capitals, he was observed climbing frantically to the top of the great pylon, camera-frame in hand, to "use up" the last streak of light. They were hard days' work; but how delightful, how rich—to him—in their result![56]

Before their return in July 1857, Frith and Wenham sent 100 stereoscopic negatives back to Negretti and Zambra in London, one of the leading publishers of foreign and local stereo views of the day.[57] Wenham may have been a consultant to this firm and probably figured decisively in the transaction.[58] Negretti and Zambra had the stereo negatives printed up as transparencies. These albumen-on-glass stereos were shown in the spring of 1857 at Photographic Society meetings in London, yet were withheld from commercial distribution for fear of piracy.[59] (In the second half of the 1850s, copyright of photographic images was still without law although cases did appear in court and were widely discussed in the photographic press.) By the fall of 1857, however, the albumen-on-glass stereos were being shown to photographers in Liverpool, where they were warmly received: "The most important and interesting views being a series of stereoscopic views from Egypt, taken by Messrs. Frith and Wenham."[60]

The stereoscopic effect was not yet thoroughly understood, and discussion of it occupied considerable space in the photographic press. Specifically, there was substantial disagreement on the amount of separation necessary between the two positions of the lenses or cameras taking the stereo pair in order to produce the illusion of spatial depth when viewed side by side.[61] Wenham gained his practical experience and expertise in Egypt with Frith, and expressed himself as an expert on this problem:

Any degree of angle that will produce the desired effect [the appearance of solidity and relative distance] is correct and advisable. . . . This I frequently [had] been obliged to do in cases where, with the *usual* angle, I could not obtain any stereoscopic effect at all.[62]

The stereos were finally published late in 1857.[63] Remarkably, *The Times* praised the views for nearly a third of a column:

> [It is] the first serious and worthy effort that has been made to develope the educational uses of the stereoscope in an artistic, geographical, and historical point of view. . . . The views are to be commended, not only for their photographic excellence but for the effective selection of the points from which they are taken.[64]

These transparent stereos were also noted in the photographic press:

> Nothing that we have seen in photography has interested us as much as this collection . . . . He is not only a skilful manipulator, but his subjects are remarkable for the judicious selection of the point of view, and observance of the time when the shadows are most effectively cast.[65]

The Athenaeum praised the stereos picturesquely:

> Mr. Frith, who makes light of everything, brings us the Sun's opinion of Egypt, which is better than Champollion's, Wilkinson's, Eōthen's, or Titmarsh's. . . . As photographs these views of Mr. Frith are worthy of special praise for their decision of touch, their sharp clear brightness, and their delicious, sunny, silvery, or twilight tone.[66]

Within this review, the incorrect information that Frith was an artist employed and sent by Negretti and Zambra was reprinted from the pamphlet accompanying the stereos. Actually, Frith had traveled on his own account and only later sold the stereo negatives to Negretti and Zambra. The larger views were handled, according to transactions executed by Frith on his return, by the printsellers Agnew[67] and for serial publication by James S. Virtue. Because Frith was far away in Palestine at this time, his sister felt compelled to respond to *The Athenaeum* on his behalf:

> [Frith went] on his own responsibility, and, independently of any suggestion from Messrs. Negretti and Zambra, or any other publishers. . . . Any credit which belongs to the selection of route or subjects is due to my brother alone.[68]

Negretti and Zambra were forced to reply:

> Mr. Frith is a gentleman of independent means, who travels for his own pleasure, and is not in any way employed by Messrs. Negretti and Zambra.[69]

This failed to end the misunderstanding for shortly, in 1862, Frith's medal-winning views were again described as "Taken for Negretti and Zambra."[70] Forty years later, and ironically only two issues before those carrying Frith's obituary notices, *The British Journal of Photography*, in discussing a revival of the stereoscope, recalled that Negretti and Zambra "sent an artist [unnamed] to Palestine and the Holy Land to take negatives."[71]

Concurrently with the publication of the stereos during the winter and spring of 1857–1858, slide shows of Frith's Egyptian—and a few Holy Land—views were held in Manchester and Liverpool. The projected size of the images was 30 by 25 feet via a regular magic lantern, creating so-called "dissolving views." Praised as an educational innovation, the shows contained 45 views including local and Continental scenes by other, unidentified, photographers. The series ran for 139 presentations, with Frith's exotic scenes clearly the hit of the show.[72]

The larger albumen prints were praised by Frith's hometown photo publication in August 1857:

> Some of Mr. Frith's, or Messrs, Frith and Wenham's views of Egypt, are remarkably fine. The plates measure 15 by 19 inches,

and we have been informed that success is attained only by repeated efforts, assiduously made, until a good negative is secured.[73]

These larger views and 100 of the 9-by-7-inch size were shown at a Manchester Photographic Society meeting in November 1857. The smaller ones were offered for sale at three shillings each. "They comprised," reported *The Liverpool and Manchester Photographic Journal*, "scenes of the highest historic and topographic interest."[74]

Reviewing the Photographic Society's 1858 exhibition at the South Kensington Museum the following February, *The Athenaeum* especially noted "Mr. Frith's burning blackness of Egyptian Shadows."[75] Frith's hometown magazine, *The Liverpool and Manchester Photographic Journal*, continued to rave about his accomplishments:

> The wonderful impress of truth, the brilliancy of the atmospheric effects, the transparency of the shadows, the perfect rendering of every point and scratch in the stone, all combine to excite an amount of pleasurable satisfaction in the spectator rarely to be surpassed.[76]

This exhibition apparently also included the first of Frith's views of Palestine sent back from the second trip that was to last well into the spring of 1858. These new photographs were reported as "admirable specimens of this artist's best manner."[77]

The art press, most attentive to photography in the late 1850s, also singled Frith out for special praise:

> The real value of photography is, however, most strikingly shown in the productions of F. Frith, jun. His subjects in Palestine and Egypt impress us with a consciousness of truth and power which no other Art-production could produce. . . . All those photographs by Mr. F. Frith should be very carefully studied.[78]

It is important to remember that while all this remarkable success was accruing in the winter of 1857–1858, Francis Frith was busily engaged on the second of his photographic expeditions. From November 1857 to May 1858 he returned to Egypt and toured the Holy Land. (Though he speaks of companions, they remain unidentified; we know that Wenham did not accompany him again.) Frith's departure for Palestine via Egypt in November 1857 was marred by a schedule misunderstanding that must have caused him considerable anxiety. The Alexandria steamer, loaded with all Frith's photographic equipment, departed from Liverpool without him. A Liverpool Photographic Society meeting noted the misfortune:

> The whole of his apparatus was on board, and would consequently arrive out before he could reach Alexandria. A strong sympathy was expressed for Mr. Frith in the annoying and vexatious dilemma in which he was placed. . . . All lovers of photography could not but wish him every success in his important undertaking.[79]

Frith's equipment probably arrived safely for he did go on to photograph Jerusalem, Damascus, Baalbek and the Cedars of Lebanon. His route from Egypt to the Holy Land was by way of the "short desert," as the sea route from Alexandria to Jaffa and overland to Jerusalem was then called.[80]

Frith may have rephotographed Cairo and the Pyramids at this time in the 7-by-9-inch format, but there is no conclusive evidence that he did so. Unlike the first 75 or so numbered negatives in the first trip's "E" series, which are inscribed "1857," the last quarter of the negatives in the "E" series are not dated at all, although they are all views of Cairo. Also, none of the views with "E" numbers in the mid 70s to upper 90s appears in the two volumes of *Egypt and Palestine*. This suggests two possibilities. Either Frith made these views on this second trip and withheld them from publication until needed in a later series, or else these high-number "E"-series views were photographed on the third trip in 1859–1860 and numbered to fit the work of several years previous. In any event, there are large, 16-by-20-inch, views of the Pyramids inscribed "Frith 1858," which suggests that Frith at least revisited those sites with some photographic equipment on this second journey eastward.[81]

About 50 7-by-9-inch views were made in Palestine on the 1857–1858 second trip. Starting with Ramleh on the route from Jaffa to Jerusalem, the inscriptions in the negatives begin "P100" and travel as far north as Baalbek and the Cedars of Lebanon. Frith wrote little about his photographic experiences in Palestine except to remark on the handy availability of rock tombs for use as dark rooms when the need arose: "Many of *my* photographic pictures were made in **TOMBS**! To save myself the trouble of pitching my dark tent, and also for the sake of their greater coolness, I very often availed myself of a rock-tomb."[82]

On this trip, Frith does seem to have been more alert to the interesting cross-cultural human interactions that are the real treats of international travel. He hunted game with local Turkish officials and was entertained in their homes, yet he remained a grudging colonialist. At Baalbek Frith photographed the small circular temple:

> The view was taken from the roof of a house, the good housewife having been bribed to admit the artist by a sum equivalent to one shilling and eight pence; but this extravagant sum by no means included "peace and quietness"—mine hostess noisily insinuating at intervals of a few minutes that for more time she required more piastres![83]

And at Hebron Frith observed the Jewish agricultural settlements making substantial progress "under the patronage of a benevolent European society."[84]

By June 1858, only one month after Frith's return to England, Negretti and Zambra had issued a series (announced in March) of 58 albumen-on-glass stereoscopic views of the Holy Land.[85] The review of these stereos in *The Athenaeum* was laudatory, despite the writer's observation that the tourist's route through the Holy Land was now traceable "by coloured posters and Bass's pale-ale corks: the signs of our presence all over the world."[86]

No longer the untried amateur, Frith was welcomed back warmly at the London Photographic Society meeting of June 1, 1858. Learning that Frith was in the room, the chairman invited him to comment on his experiences with photographic chemistry in a hot climate, the topic then under discussion at the gathering. "After being rapturously cheered" by the members, Frith spoke at length on his experiences with photography in extreme heat. While his remarks are ostensibly technical, they reveal the pleasure and excitement of an artistic sensibility:

> The correct time in the exposure of the picture is the most important. I believe, with a very good collodion film, sensitized with the iodine of cadmium, a good developing solution will produce a picture always. I found a difficulty in Nubia and Egypt, from the heat of the climate. I found that my nitrate of silver bath was very much more active; and in some instances, when the thermometer was 120° or 130° in my tent, an immersion of half a minute was sufficient; with a longer immersion, the plate lost sensitiveness. I confess I am extremely careless, and scarcely know often what I use; at the same time, with

ordinary materials, I scarcely ever fail to produce a picture of some sort. I do not prefer to work rapidly upon a landscape, from which I may pass away for ever, but rather slowly; for if you are working with rapid collodion, half a second more or less exposure may spoil your picture. I prefer taking about forty seconds.[87]

Throughout his writings, in self-conscious hyperbole, there are charming (yet culture-bound) expressions of Frith's delight with expeditionary photography:

> As for your artist, his clearest recollections are of a luxurious and effective field-day hereaway, for he rigged up his photographic tent in the small boat, and was pulled about by his shiny black Nubians from dawn till dusk, just landing and knocking off a view wherever and whenever the fancy struck him. Ah, brother Photographers! with a sky like *that*, and such subjects, and a bottle of splendid pale—not ale—but, collodion, you only can imagine the glory of such a day.[88]

> Philae is the most beautiful thing in Egypt; . . . I flatter myself, too, somewhat upon the quality of my Photograph—light transparent shadows, sweet half-tones, oh discriminating Public![89]

Yet, Frith's days were not all sunlight and high spirits; witness his description of the Nubian temple interior he used as a darkroom early in his first trip:

> I prepared my pictures by candle-light in one of the interior chambers of the temple. It was a most unpleasant apartment—the hole in which I worked. The floor was covered to the depth of several inches with an impalpable, ill-flavoured dust, which rose in clouds as we moved; from the roof were suspended groups of fetid bats—the most offensively smelling creatures in existence.[90]

By the end of his second trip, Frith seems to have been thoroughly at ease in the Middle East. In Damascus, he was again prompted to use the most ecstatic language:

> Attempt not, I beseech thee, to square those door-panels or window-frames with the straight-edge of thine eye (in the East there are no straight lines, no squares, no circles); the shade is welcome, the green of the orange and rose trees is refreshing; blue and gold are beautiful colors; believe, smoke, and be happy![91]

Frith also wrote tellingly of his developing photographic aesthetic. He loved the truthfulness of photography too much to consider becoming an artist in traditional media. Though he envied painters their freedom to compose—and did himself take up painting later in his life—he believed that his artistic control as a photographer was entirely, if reluctantly, subordinate to his camera:

> I shall endeavour to make the simple truthfulness of the Camera a guide for my Pen. . . . A photographer only knows—only he can appreciate the difficulty of getting a view satisfactorily into the camera: foregrounds are especially perverse; distance too near or too far; the falling away of the ground; the intervention of some brick wall or other commonplace object, which an artist would simply *omit*; some or all of these things (with plenty others of a similar character) are the rule, not the exception. I have often thought, when manoeuvring about for a position for my camera, of the exclamation of the great mechanist of antiquity—"Give me a fulcrum for my lever, and I will move the world." Oh what pictures we would make, if we could command our points of view![92]

In an essay of compositional analysis and apology, Frith granted Truth the victory over Beauty:

> It is true that the temple [at Philae] outdoes the Tower of Babel, not only "reaching unto the heavens," but robbing the

picture of well-nigh all its sky—that feature so essential to the picturesque in landscape. But what could I do? I *must* give that scrap of water, and the Nile boat . . . and I could not falsify the height of the bank, as I see most artists have done, to suit the proportions of my picture.[93]

And occasionally Frith's attitude bordered on the defensive, as when he photographed at Karnak:

I believe that this obelisk is the most beautiful in Egypt. . . . Around is a perfect chaos of splendid ruin, amongst which I found it extremely difficult to fix my instruments so as to command a view. May he who finds fault with the arrangement of the picture be dragged to the spot, and compelled to find a better point![94]

It is interesting to note that Frith's fussiness about his own visual choices and adaptations occurs mostly with the photos from the first Egyptian trip. Though the texts in *Egypt and Palestine* may have been written sequentially as published, i.e. in no geographical order whatsoever, the Palestine views, made after Frith had received considerable public praise and success, seem to have evoked much less self-conscious memories. The texts accompanying them are more descriptive of the content of the photographs, and when personal, the comments are more narrative and less exclamatory.

Only twice did Frith discuss the qualities of his pictures, besides "truthfulness," that are unique to photography. He complained of his disappointment with the wretched reality of the city of Damascus and wondered whether this totality of reality "is revealed by Photography to an extent to which we are unaccustomed in art, that its effect is rarely quite gratifying to the eye?" Contrarily, Frith acknowledged that his "desire is to convey truthful impressions."[95] And yet, on occasion, he seems to have felt himself to be an adversary to his equipment:

This is one of the few views which a photograph can render without, perhaps, greatly detracting from its artistic fame. . . . the Sun himself condescends to pigmify it, and pop it bodily into the box which your artist provided.[96]

Early in 1858, while Frith was still in the Holy Land on his second photographic expedition, the first subscription issue of *Egypt and Palestine* was released.[97] James S. Virtue, publisher of this series as well as of *The Art Journal*, placed an enticing announcement for it in that magazine's January 1858 news columns, heralding it as "An Experiment in Photography."[98] The official review in *The Art Journal*, written after four issues had appeared, opened with words echoing Frith's: "We have before us the very best work we have ever yet met with, to illustrate two of the most interesting countries in the world."[99] Considering that Frith's book and this magazine were published by the same person, the review seems remarkably fair. The reviewer, taking a traditional aesthetic interpretation, sympathized with point-of-view and perspective "problems" endemic to photography, yet prophetically held that where facts were wanted, such photographically illustrated books would replace those of the engraver.[100]

The whole 25-part, 76-print production that was *Egypt and Palestine* was completed in the spring of 1860, in an edition of 2000. It was favorably reviewed as a major photographic event: "It will no more be possible to do without photography than without the printing press" was the most insightful of the many comments greeting the series' completion.[101] In a format also followed in subsequent publications, the albumen prints in *Egypt and Palestine* were mounted on heavy stock with printed titles and the legend "Frith Photo." One reviewer recommended rebinding the 76 prints and their texts in geo-graphical order to avoid the "pillar to post" manner in which the various subjects were issued.[102]

Frith's production methods for photographic permanence were praised and recommended as a paradigm of modern printing practice. The Reigate firm of F. Frith & Co. was ready to contribute further to the refinement of photographic printing for book illustrations in addition to their regular output. The questionable permanence of some silver prints, evidenced by fading blacks and yellowing highlights, continued to plague less careful photographers. Frith felt he had no choice as long as ink or pigment substitutes remained unsatisfactory replacements. Obviously keeping up with current photography, pioneer W. H. Fox Talbot in 1858 used Frith's stereo image of the Edfu temple to demonstrate his own experimental photoglyph process.[103] An attempt at permanence, this screened or grained intaglio ink process never advanced to the mass-production stage. Frith had also tried carbon printing—another, more successful "permanent" process, then in its infancy—without achieving convincing results and had given it up by 1859 as hopeless for general purposes.[104]

The mass-production operation at the Reigate studio and the absolute irreplaceability of the original glass negatives necessitated the use of copy negatives for the actual production of albumen prints. The near grainless quality of collodion plates permitted this copying without a perceptible loss of detail in the finished image. Some of these (apparently) working negatives showed considerably sophisticated masking and retouching.[105] Yet the final prints are remarkably free of the harsh or strident effects of such manipulation. Indeed, Frith's high technical skill seems to have served him as well in the studio as it did in the deserts of the Middle East.

Following the enthusiastic reception of his publication and his congratulatory welcome home in June 1858, Frith spent over a year in England furthering his projects and preparing for one last journey east. The period 1858–1859 was also hectic with exhibitions of Frith's photographs in all parts of Britain. The large views of Egypt were shown at the Photographic Society of Scotland and praised for their size as lending a "grandeur to his subjects in the present exhibition which was previously wanting."[106] Frith's "panorama" of Cairo was of great interest. Shown at Suffolk Street in January 1859, it consisted of seven prints mounted side by side, with a total area of eight and a half feet by 20 inches. It created a small sensation: "His mosques, and pyramids and Eastern streets leave nothing but colour to be desired."[107] Reportedly the panorama was later to be presented to Muhammed Said Pasha of Egypt as an expression of gratitude for his assistance to Frith and Wenham.[108] Previously this panorama had appeared side by side with scenes of Cairo by Robertson and Beato at the Architectural Photographic Association exhibition in Pall Mall—to Frith's great advantage. As one reviewer stated: "It is almost a matter of surprise that anyone should have attempted to photograph Cairo so soon after Frith had done it."[109] Frith also served on the Association's committee for distributing photographic prints to members and, as might be imagined, his work was in great demand that season.[110]

The late 1850s were bright years for photography. Never again in the century would such diverse periodicals as *The Athenaeum*, *The Art Journal* and *Notes and Queries* pay such serious attention to individual photographers and annual exhibitions. Only in 1859 could *The Photographic Journal* quote lavishly from the daily press's praise of the generally high quality of the Photographic Society's exhibition, held that year at Suffolk Street.[111] The location was noteworthy because Suffolk Street was traditionally the site of fine painting exhibitions. For this one light-filled year, photography was allowed to hang in those prestigious rooms. *Notes and Queries,* long a friend of photography, saluted its success in its exhibition review:

> The collection of works exhibited shows the steady and gradual improvement of this important Art. When in its infancy, we stepped out of our way, and made "N. & Q." a channel of photographic information: we did so under the feeling that the importance of the Art to the cause of pictorial Truth was not sufficiently recognized by any of our contemporaries. We may be permitted to look back in satisfaction, when we see, as in the present Exhibition, how our anticipations of its future importance and development have been realized.[112]

It must have been a heady time for Frith. His work was famous and admired—so much so that reports of pirating and unauthorized sales of Frith prints formed part of the evidence recommending copyright for photographs.[113] In March 1859 an article by Frith called "The Art of Photography" appeared in *The Art Journal.* His opening paragraphs assume that art lovers have accepted photography as a legitimate, if infant, "pictorial" art equal to the steel engraving or lithography of the day.[114] As this seems to be Frith's only formal statement to a sophisticated art audience, his thoughts are worth quoting at some length.

Frith believed the major attribute of photography that explained its popularity was "its *essential* truthfulness of outline, and, to a considerable extent, of perspective, and light and shade." He insisted that this truthfulness to nature, in a popular art, was highly moral, designating it a "*spiritual quality* . . . , a charm of freshness and power, which was quite independent of general or artistic effect, and which appeals to our readiest sympathies." Aware that one of the perils of easy production was shoddy or wretched images, Frith admitted that the mechanical aspect of photography was a two-edged sword:

> The student [photographer] should bear in mind that what he has to aim at is not the production of a large number of *good* pictures, but if possible, of *one* that shall satisfy all the requirements of his judgment and taste.
>
> Think of the careful thought and labour which are expended over every successful piece of canvas, and the months of patient work which are requisite to perfect a first-class steel plate! and then turn to the gentleman who describes a machine which he has contrived for taking six dozen pictures a day! Every one of them—this is the distressing part of the business—every one of them capable of throwing off as many impressions as a steel plate! We shudder to think of the thousands of vile "negatives" boxed up at this moment in holes and corners, any one of which may, on a sunny day, hatch a brood of hateful "positives."
>
> We feel it to be a solemn duty to remind photographers of the responsibilities which they incur by harbouring these dangerous reproductive productions; and we beg of them—for their own sakes, and for that of society—to lose no time in washing off or otherwise destroying, by far the greater part of these "negative" productions.

"Image pollution" seems to have been a pitfall early recognized as basic to the nature of photography, and was, like other environmental pollutions, endemic to the rise of high technology.

Frith also believed that there were transcendent qualities to an artist's work no matter what medium was used:

> To practice the Art [photography] *with distinction,* which will very shortly be, if it be not now, the only kind of practice which will command notice, requires a much greater acquaintance with the principles of Art than would seem to be applicable to a "merely mechanical science." . . .

> We do not believe in its power to deter any youth, to whom nature has given an artist's eye and heart, from a proper cultivation of those tastes and talents with which he is gifted. Your most accomplished artist, if he will stoop to the task, will ever be your best photographer; and your skilful "manipulator," if he be possessed likewise of a grain of sense or perception, will never rest until he has acquainted himself with the rules which are applied to Art in its higher walks; and he will then make it his constant and most anxious study how he can apply these rules to his own pursuit.

Written a decade before his firm achieved its status as the most prolific of the English photo-view concerns, and at a time when his own photographs of English scenery were being less-than-favorably compared to his Middle Eastern views,[115] Frith's 1859 *Art Journal* article is prophetic, perhaps self-critical, and certainly naïvely optimistic.

In that same article, Frith supplied the beginnings of a history of photography, but a second promised essay is not to be found. The non-appearance of the rest of Frith's projected work for *The Art Journal* is curious indeed and in some way parallels a general and inexplicably precipitous decline in the amount of attention devoted to photography by the literary and art press. After a long and steady increase in the coverage of photographic events and figures, culminating in the congratulatory attitudes of 1859, English periodicals of 1860 and afterward largely ignore the topics. In retrospect, the cheering salutation quoted previously from *Notes and Queries* early in 1859 had proved sadly premature. The low point in this decline was reached in the 1862 International Exhibition, where English photography was classed for display and judging along with "Philosophical Instruments" and was exhibited in the dank and leaky upper galleries of the Crystal Palace. The scandal occupied much of the photographic literature for the first half of 1862.

However, the account is getting ahead of itself, for none of this had yet happened when Frith began his third and final trip to the Middle East. Surely, he felt confident and enthusiastic as he set out in the late summer of 1859 to revisit Egypt and the Holy Land—scenes to which he knew he would probably not return again. His last text concerning his favorite spot, the island of Philae, is a poem that begins, "'Tis hard to leave thee, Legendary Isle!"[116]

More importantly, Frith's third and final expedition took him to places never before visited by the camera. Traveling by camel, Frith passed south along the Nile to an area between the Second and Third Cataracts which was at that time considered the northernmost section of Ethiopia. Wadi Halfa, at the Second Cataract, was thought of as the border between Nubia and Ethiopia. Frith's scholarly authority for the southernmost portion of the trip was George Alexander Hoskins, whose *Travels in Ethiopia; Above the Second Cataract of the Nile* (1835) recounted his 1833 expedition to the ancient kingdom of Meroë above the Fifth Cataract. Hoskins, on a return trip to Egypt in 1859–1861, could have seen Frith among the photographers there as he noted that "Photographic machines have superseded the pencil in delineating the monuments"— although he recommended his favorite local watercolorist to the truly serious view buyer![117]

Frith's goal in "Ethiopia" was Soleb and its Temple of Amenophis III. Although one reviewer referred to these views of Frith's as being from "above the Sixth Cataract of the Nile,"[118] Soleb is downriver from the Third Cataract! Frith's published books contain no photos from areas south of this location. In fact, the southernmost point of ancient Egyptian occupation, and hence monuments, is Kurgus, between the

Fourth and the Fifth Cataracts. Even so, Frith reported that at Soleb he was told he was the first European visitor in five years.[119] Frith made the "Ethiopian" trek in January 1860 over a period of 18 days, arriving in Soleb on day six. He had to journey less encumbered than previously, and seems to have left the big plate camera at Wadi Halfa. The whole-plate and stereo outfits were quite enough to manage on camel: "I carried as little luggage as possible—my photographic 'impedimenta' being the chief of it—but my little black operating-tent served to cover me by night."[120]

Before his departure that summer of 1859, the Collodion Committee of the Photographic Society had given Frith some experimental collodion to test which had been especially formulated for work in hot climates. In an informal communication to the Committee from Cairo in August 1859, Frith announced that he was able to make exposures in four to five seconds on full-size plates:

> I have some hope of getting an interesting series of instantaneous pictures, by using a stop of 1½ inches in diameter on the portrait lens (3¼ inches in diameter). The lens then covers a 4½ inch plate with tolerable depth of focus, and I can obtain a sufficiently developed picture with an absolutely instantaneous exposure, sailing boats with the ropes sharp, moving figures, &c.[121]

Curiously, these four-and-a-half-inch views were not included in any of Frith's photographic-view books.

Adverse field conditions persisted, especially in August:

> We have just returned, after having spent five days in the mud house of an artist at the Pyramids, where we were devoured by thousands of sandflies; the water very bad and the heat great. I worked hard, and took some fine pictures. I still get landscapes with the smallest aperture of the view lens in four seconds, and have taken capital pictures in the heat of the day. I should imagine the temperature in my little tent could not be less than 130° Fahrenheit; the developing solution was quite hot.[122]

The fastidious negative-numbering of the first two trips was somewhat abandoned on this last expedition. An inventory of the published photographs and their negative inscriptions in light of their dates of publication has allowed some pattern to emerge. There is a sequence without letter prefixes that continues the numbering used in the Holy Land "P" series; this unprefixed series covers, in order, Cairo and environs, the Sinai and Jerusalem. The negatives from the long trip down the Nile were unnumbered, but signed, and include some Cairo views and all points of interest below Cairo down to Soleb in "Ethiopia." A series of 100 stereo views was also made on this trip down the Nile.

Frith was able to rephotograph many familiar monuments. Medinet Habu, at Thebes, had been recently excavated. While there, Frith encountered a French artist copying its details:

> When in a few minutes, I had possessed myself of more accuracy than his labour of perhaps days would yield, he exclaimed with politeness—and (let us hope) with no dash of bitterness, nor scornfulness, nor envy—"Ah, Monsieur! que vous êtes vite, vite!"[123]

Frith returned to Karnak as well, stalking the interior like a hunter after prey:

> Then, burning with ambition—yet with much fearfulness—I entered that dark vista . . . and turning down one of the side aisles, I pointed my camera at a double line of those dingy old immensities—indestructible—indescribable, and hitherto deemed impossible![124]

Returning from the "Ethiopian" trip, Frith photographed in Cairo for the last time before setting out for Palestine, his route this time being over the "long desert" (see note 81). The whole trek took 40 days on camel. Several of the Sinai views show the group's encampments in the desert. After traveling as far north as Jerusalem and rephotographing its relics, Frith boarded a steamer at Jaffa and slowly made his way home, touring the Bosporus, Constantinople, Smyrna and the Greek islands.[125]

MORE PHOTOGRAPHIC BOOKS

Following his return in 1860, Frith produced nine more books of photographs using views from the different series taken on all three trips. Yet, strangely, the amount of critical notice generated by all his subsequent publishing activity seems to be in inverse proportion to the volume of Frith's output. Indeed, the decline of outside interest in photographs noted above is suggested in part by such silence. The photographic press continued to notice Frith and accord him some attention as one of the masters among English topographic photographers. However, even the photography journals noted the increasing popularity, and hence declining remarkability, of Egypt and the Holy Land as destinations for expeditionary photographers. Already reflecting this development in late 1859, a review of Negretti and Zambra stereos of the Philippines observed: "In proportion as the appearance of the camera became more common in Egypt and the Holy Land, the more adventurous photographers turned their steps to more distant and less known countries."[126]

While Frith was still in the Middle East, his publisher, James S. Virtue, released the final part of *Egypt and Palestine Photographed and Described by Francis Frith*. Inside was a flyer announcing a new series, based on photos from Frith's last expedition, entitled *Cairo, Sinai, Jerusalem, and the Pyramids of Egypt*. The ambitious 20-part, 60-print series is uniform with *Egypt and Palestine* and forms a sequel to it. (The numbering of all 60 negatives fits into that of the third trip, already discussed; no earlier "E" or "P" series views appear.) However, Frith was not the author of the descriptive letterpress; rather, the series was now emphasizing history and archaeology. The authors of the page-long texts were Mrs. Sophia Poole, whose *The Englishwoman in Egypt; Letters from Cairo* (1844–1846) was quite well known, and her younger son, Reginald Stuart Poole, then an assistant in the Department of Antiquities at the British Museum. It is probably this team that is quoted anonymously on the flyer:

> The value of a photograph—its principal charm at least—is its infallible *truthfulness*. We may have long revelled in the *poetry* of the East; but this work enables us to look, as it were, upon its realities. We have reason to be grateful to the men whose genius has entertained and delighted us (from the author of the "Arabian Nights" downwards), but it is satisfactory and interesting now to have the silken veil withdrawn, and allow the sun himself to reveal to us the sculptured mysteries of grand old Egypt, and the desolation of modern Palestine.

The value of such photographs and the fulfilling of Arago's claim is stated in the publisher's blurb on the back cover of Part One:

> No drawing, however carefully executed, has enabled an orientalist to read the intricate and sometimes foreshortened inscriptions on mosques and tombs, which has been done in many instances for the descriptions of this work.

The beginning of the Civil War in the United States may account for Virtue's New York office issuing only Part One of *Cairo, Sinai, Jerusalem, and the Pyramids of Egypt* and no more. In England, the whole subscription probably ran for more than a year. As the title states, the pyramids of Giza and Dahshur are the southernmost monuments of this particular collection; Frith's 1859–1860 long trip down the Nile appears in a later series.

Sometime after the Pooles contributed their authoritative though opinionated text, their words (and some new paragraphs) were matched to 20 of the very large views taken on the three trips. That volume, or portfolio, *Egypt, Sinai, and Jerusalem,* was published by William Mackenzie of London and Glasgow in 1860–1861. It was also issued by Virtue in 1862 in ten parts of two photos each, for 21 shillings per part. The Pooles' preface reiterates their belief that photography is the best medium for communicating accurately the landscape of archaeology or history: "The manner in which the forms are given, and the successful rendering of the distance . . . at once seize the eye." It is interesting to note that only two of the 20 photos included are of Sinai, and only one is of Jerusalem.

Frith was in Egypt in January 1860 and so did not show any work at the Photographic Society exhibition that winter. However, his previous *Egypt and Palestine* series plus the Cairo panorama were exhibited (along with photos by Roger Fenton, O. J. Rejlander and H. P. Robinson, and other paintings and engravings) at a Liverpool Society of Fine Arts exhibition in May.[127] Otherwise, there was little activity until the fall of 1860, following Frith's return, when the Crystal Palace display of Egyptian manufactures was graced with Frith's latest views of the Middle East.[128]

Curiously, as in 1860, Frith again failed to exhibit at the Photographic Society in January 1861. Instead, he seems to have concentrated his energy on the soon-to-be-defunct Architectural Photographic Association (ceased October 1861)[129] and its exhibition at the Architectural Union Company. Showing 31 new Egyptian views to the expected favorable reviews, he was commended for including newly excavated works at Thebes.[130] Frith's last formal exhibition of his Middle Eastern series was probably at the International Exhibition of 1862, where British photography was so shabbily treated. Even so, his photographs—shown as "Views in the East"—were still highly regarded as "work which has done more to make known the aspect of Egyptian, Syrian and other countries, than all the volumes of word-painting that have been produced on the subject."[131]

Actually, instead of exhibiting widely upon his final return home, Frith probably spent the end of 1860 and the next year getting married and preparing to start family life on his own—undertakings which he termed "life in earnest."[132] His bride was Mary Ann Rosling, the 22-year-old daughter of his Quaker neighbors in Reigate.[133] The Friths had eight children during their long and contented marriage. As Frith began to specialize in views of the British countryside, photographic expeditions became occasions for family excursions. During the earliest years of the 1860s Frith was also furthering the interests of his photographic-view business in Reigate.

Early in 1862, *The Photographic Journal* announced the publication of a Bible by the firm Eyre and Spottiswoode illustrated with 20 views by Frith,[134] and made this special note of the significance of such a photographically illustrated text:

> The interest attaching to this work, to those who are interested in seeing the scenes of which they have so often read as they really are, can hardly be estimated; especially as Mr. Frith's

knowledge and his artistic perceptions have led him to select the best possible point of view.[135]

This Bible sold for seven pounds seven shillings (that is, seven guineas), which compared favorably with Frith's regularly priced portfolio.

Only a month later, *The Photographic Journal* reported again on Frith's activities with these dramatic words: "The extent of Mr. Frith's publications is becoming almost alarming."[136] The occasion was the publication by Smith, Elder & Co. of Frith's 1859–1860 stereos in a book titled *Egypt, Nubia, and Ethiopia* with descriptions and wood engravings by Joseph Bonomi and notes by Samuel Sharpe. Joseph Bonomi was an artist, Middle East traveler and curator from 1861 of Sir John Soane's Museum. His illustrations accompany many of the English-language publications on Egypt of his day. In fact, he had given a lecture on Frith's Egyptian views in January 1861 during the exhibition of the Architectural Photographic Association.[137] Samuel Sharpe was a scholar, Egyptologist and Biblical translator who often enlisted Bonomi's draftsmanship in his own numerous publications. The scholar in author Sharpe seemed to appreciate the photographs for their compelling documentary qualities: "Here we have all the truthfulness of nature, all the reality of the objects themselves, and, at the same time, artistic effects which leave us nothing to wish for."[138]

Later that summer the publication won a medal as part of Negretti and Zambra's exhibit at the International Exhibition for its adaptation of photography to book illustration.[139] *The Photographic Journal* called the book "a marvel of typographic and illustrative art."[140] Although it was neither the first nor the last volume to be illustrated with stereo pairs for use with a book stereoscope ("fit for the drawing-room table, price 5s. and upwards"), it was probably the largest: "The mention of one hundred stereoscopic views as illustrations to a volume will of itself serve to give some idea of the enterprising spirit with which this noble volume is put forth."[141] *The Daily Telegraph* singled the volume out for comment when it was on display in the Negretti and Zambra section of the International Exhibition that summer: "a work of high merit and interest . . . chiefly notable as a wonder of photography."[142] *The Art Journal* made a special point of praising the collaboration of the artist-traveler, the scholar and the photographer.[143]

Frith's fame that summer as *the* photographer of Egypt earned him a good-natured cartoon in the June 7, 1862 issue of *Punch.* Though disguised in the caption as "Jones," the photographer who is depicted confronting a skeptical Sphinx sports Frith's beard and floppy fez: "The great difficulty in Photography is to get the Sitter to assume a Pleasing Expression of Countenance—Jones, however, thinks that, in this instance, he has been extremely successful."

If *The Photographic Journal* was "alarmed" by the output of early 1862, they were surely stunned by what was to follow. (That in fact may be the best explanation for the virtual absence of Frith and his last five collections of Middle East views from contemporary photographic and literary journals!) Frith next published photographs for a lavish two-volume Bible to honor Queen Victoria. William Mackenzie of Glasgow printed the text in 1862–1863, in an edition of 170 unnumbered copies; price, 50 guineas. The mounts for the photos are printed with a chapter and verse citation tying the illustrated scene directly to a Biblical context. Called *The Queen's Bible* on the first title pages of both volumes, the set is bound in high-relief red morocco with thistle, rose and shamrock motifs, gold stamping, and gilt-metal edging nailed to the front and back covers. Stamped metal thistles act as clasps. Inside, the thistle, rose and shamrock motifs are repeated in the gold-stamped morocco borders of the marbleized end papers. Each volume fits snugly into a red plush-lined mahogany case with brass fittings. The whole production is a tour-de-force of Victorian design and taste. The 56 photographs bound inside come from all three of Frith's trips and are among the handsomest of the hundreds of views made on these journeys.

Frith's next project, a four-volume, 148-albumen-print reissue of the *Egypt and Palestine* and *Cairo, Sinai, Jerusalem, and the Pyramids of Egypt* photos, was probably undertaken after his original glass stereos and other views were awarded a prize medal at the 1862 International Exhibition in London, as the award is engraved as part of the design of the second title page of each volume.[144] The format is uniform with his earlier publications; the volumes were offered initially by subscription. However, perhaps heeding the earlier criticism of his previous books' random geographic order, or perhaps just finding a new approach to the same photographs, Frith has arranged the views by region: *Sinai and Palestine; Lower Egypt, Thebes, and the Pyramids; Upper Egypt and Ethiopia;* and *Egypt, Sinai, and Palestine. Supplementary Volume.* (This four-volume set was the source of the pictures in the present volume.) Each first title page is engraved, the words arching over a trimmed mounted photograph of some appropriate locale. The "Supplementary Volume," like the first part of *Egypt and Palestine,* includes a portrait of Frith himself lounging in his Turkish summer costume.[145] The texts are mostly reprints of those appearing with the same or similar views in earlier volumes. Those on "Ethiopia" are new, and Frith inserted comments and updated information in the other texts as was relevant.

Frith's firm continued to offer the Egyptian and Palestine views for sale singly or in groups for at least the rest of the century. There were other, less spectacular portfolios of selected views available with Frith's imprint, but they seem not to have been treated or preserved as discrete units. Rather, it is the books that have come down to us today. During the rest of the decade, Frith settled down to regular family life. He published a few more photo-illustrated books, among them an interesting edition of Longfellow's *Hyperion* (1865) with pictures made on a trip with Mrs. Frith retracing the hero's European travels. Otherwise, Frith was content to expand the view concern to Continental and American as well as English subjects, using hired photographers who sent their work back to the printing studio in Reigate. Negatives were no longer signed; the blind stamp "Frith's Series" on the print surface became the company's trademark. As the decades passed, Frith spent more time on religious and philosophical concerns and continued to write and publish. In his later years he also took up landscape painting.

In March 1898, *The British Journal of Photography* noted Frith's passing at his winter home in Cannes. A week later the editors caught up with the gentleman's significance for photography and wrote:

The late Mr. Francis Frith, whose death we noticed last week, while actively engaged in artistic pursuits, gained many distinctions, including that of being the first person to take a camera up the Nile, where he used it to great purpose.[146]

Forty years had dulled the memory of Firth's accomplishment and also permitted the complete obscurity of his predecessors as photographers of Egypt. Ironically, Frith's albumen-on-glass stereographs had been shown, anonymously, as venerable relics at the Historical Exhibition held that very winter in the Crystal Palace.[147] Erroneously, Frith was described, unnamed, as an "artist . . . sent to Palestine and the Holy Land" by Negretti and Zambra. It is as if the late nineteenth-century commercial-photography world of hired camera "operators" and powerful publishers were incapable of recognizing photographer Frith's enterprising and individual adventurousness.

The management of F. Frith & Co.—increasingly concentrating on postcards and printed views—passed to Frith's children and their descendants until 1968, when the studios and their contents were sold; the purchaser was insolvent by early 1971. The remaining photographic contents of the company's headquarters are recognized as a treasure trove of bygone Victorian life in Great Britain. Sadly, the collodion negatives of the ruins of Egypt and the relics of Palestine have themselves become photographic ruins.[148] Many pre-1886 glass-plate negatives, including the Middle East views, had been smashed with hammers to make concrete for an outhouse floor at the studio. Others, including some of the 16-by-20-inch Egyptian plates, had been stored and forgotten outdoors in the firm's garden. Exposure to the elements had damaged some of them beyond recovery. (Two dozen or so mammoth plates that survived are currently in New York, the property of collector Janet Lehr.) At the time of liquidation in 1971, photo historian Bill Jay persuaded Rothmans International to buy the extant collection of English views as a preservation gesture. Most recently John Buck has purchased the archive collection and will operate it as a commercial picture agency in Finchampstead, Berkshire. While European and Asian locales are also named among the surviving prints, the two ancient lands of Egypt and Palestine are absent from the inventory.[149]

Of course there is no reliving the awe and wonder with which Victorian viewers greeted Frith's startlingly truthful photographs of the most ancient and historic lands known to them. For a modern comparison, there are photographs from the moon and the planets which have had an equivalent effect on contemporary observers. Yet, even as in Frith's day, the wondrous and exotic have become the familiar in less than a decade.

The optical truth of Frith's photographs to his subjects was still a remarkable and praiseworthy quality in the late 1850s; today that is an obvious and assumed function of the photographic medium. Rather it is his exuberant command of light and shade and his authoritative communication of the solid physicality of monumental architecture—aspects of Frith's photographs which were never more compelling than in his Egypt and Holy Land views—that continue to merit admiration.

NOTES TO THE INTRODUCTION

Books and articles listed in the Bibliography are referred to here in abbreviated form.
The opening *"The"* of journal titles has been omitted.

[1] "Introduction," *Egypt and Palestine,* I.

[2] Gernsheim & Gernsheim, *History of Photography,* p. 285.

[3] Jay, *Victorian Cameraman,* p. 7.

[4] "Photography: The Francis Frith Collection," *ARTnewsletter,* III (Nov. 1, 1977), p. 5.

[5] Unless otherwise noted, Jay, pp. 9–16, is the source for most of Frith's pre-1856 biography.

[6] Frith was described as a printer; the other two professional members were a photographer and a photo supplier and lensmaker (Good, *History of the Liverpool Amateur Photographic Association,* pp. 6–7 illus.).

[7] *Liverpool Photographic Journal,* III (Mar. 8, 1856), p. 29.

[8] Darrah, *World of Stereographs,* p. 108 illus.

[9] Jay, p. 28, refers to it as an 1858 publication. While Frith could have taken the Cambridge scenes anytime, he is only credited in the book itself with printing them.

[10] "Doum Palm, and Ruined Mosque, Near Philae," *Egypt and Palestine,* II.

[11] "Introduction," *Egypt and Palestine,* I.

[12] The title was ancient Greek for "from the east."

[13] "Introduction," *Egypt and Palestine,* I.

[14] *Liverpool Photographic Journal,* III (Jan. 12, 1856), p. 1.

[15] "Bethlehem, and the Church of the Nativity," *Egypt and Palestine,* II.

[16] "The Great Columns and Smaller Temple, Baalbec," *Egypt and Palestine,* I.

[17] "Nazareth, from the North-west," *Sinai and Palestine.*

[18] For example: Dawson & Uphill, *Who Was Who in Egyptology,* and Wortham, *Genesis of British Egyptology.*

[19] "The Granite Pylon, &c., Karnac," *Egypt and Palestine,* II.

[20] See especially: Bull & Lorimor, *Up the Nile*; Jammes & Jammes, "Egypt in Flaubert's Time"; and Darrah, *World of Stereographs,* pp. 130–31 illus.

[21] Arago, "Le Daguerréotype," p. 256.

[22] Jenson & Wister, "The Big Picture," p. 112.

[23] Gernsheim & Gernsheim, *History of Photography,* p. 116 illus.

[24] Flaubert's diaries and letters from this three-year expedition have been published in several French editions; English-language readers will enjoy *Flaubert in Egypt,* translated and edited by Francis Steegmuller.

[25] This roughly 6-by-9-inch format was rivaled by much larger prints of Egyptian subjects, 18 by 14 inches, such as those offered in 1854 by Bland & Long of London, photographer(s) unspecified; see Bland & Long, *Catalogue of Apparatus & Chemical Preparations Used in the Art of Photography,* p. 84, issued in Charles A. Long, *Practical Photography on Glass and Paper.*

[26] Jammes & Jammes, "Egypt in Flaubert's Time," p. 64.

[27] *Athenaeum,* XXXI (June 5, 1858), p. 727; *Photographic Notes,* II (Dec. 1, 1857), p. 442.

[28] Jammes & Jammes, "Egypt in Flaubert's Time," p. 64.

[29] *Photographic Journal,* V (Jan. 8, 1858), p. 131.

[30] *Athenaeum,* XXXIII (Feb. 26, 1859), p. 290, and XXXIV (Feb. 18, 1860), p. 243; *Photographic News,* III (Mar. 2, 1860), pp. 313–14, 319.

[31] *The British Journal of Photography* contains progress reports of the tour and the book throughout 1862. See also *Photographic News,* VI (July 11, 1862), p. 336; (July 25, 1862), pp. 351–52.

[32] *Photographic Journal,* VIII (July 15, 1862), pp. 81, 83, 85.

[33] Palgrave, "A Visit to Upper Egypt," p. 253.

[34] Gernsheim & Gernsheim, *History of Photography,* pp. 132, 562.

[35] See also: John Cramb, "Notes of a Photographic Tour in the Holy Land," *British Journal of Photography,* VI & VII (1859–1860), in 15 installments; his "Palestine in 1860; or, A Photographer's Journal of a Visit to Jerusalem," *British Journal of Photography,* VII & VIII (1860–1861), in 12 installments; and *Photographic News,* VI (July 25, 1862), p. 355.

[36] *Photographic Notes,* IV (Nov. 9, 1860), p. 336.

[37] "News and Notes," *Palestine Exploration Quarterly,* CX (July–Dec. 1978), pp. 73–74.

[38] Jammes & Jammes, p. 63, also point this out.

[39] "Introduction," *Egypt and Palestine,* I.

[40] *Photographic Journal,* IV (Feb. 22, 1858), p. 159.

[41] *British Journal of Photography,* IX (Oct. 1, 1862), p. 368.

[42] "Doum Palm, and Ruined Mosque, Near Philae," *Egypt and Palestine,* II.

[43] *Egypt and Palestine,* II.

[44] "Cairo, from the East," in Poole & Poole, *Cairo, Sinai, Jerusalem, and the Pyramids of Egypt.*

[45] "The Pyramids of Sakkárah, from the North-east," in Poole & Poole, *Egypt, Sinai, and Jerusalem.*

[46] "The Temple of El-Karnac, from the South-east," in Poole & Poole, *Egypt, Sinai, and Jerusalem.*

[47] The small view appears as "'Pharaoh's Bed,' Island of Philae," *Egypt and Palestine,* I; the large view, as "The Hypaethral Temple, Philae," in the Pooles' *Egypt, Sinai, and Jerusalem.*

[48] Hardwich, "Reminiscences"; cf. Welling, *Photography in America,* pp. 123–26, 408.

[49] *Photographic Journal,* III (May 21, 1856), p. 52.

[50] Frith mentions no specific photo authority; however, two respected contemporary handbooks that he could have used stress this point, the Thornthwaite *Guide to Photography* and the Hardwich *Manual of Photographic Chemistry.*

[51] "Tiberias, from the South," *Egypt and Palestine,* II.

[52] "Early Morning at Wady Kardassy, Nubia," *Egypt and Palestine,* II.

[53] F. H. Wenham, *Aerial Locomotion,* ed. by T. O'B. Hubbard & J. L. Ledeboer (London: Aeronautical Society of Great Britain, 1910); reprinted from Aeronautical Society, *First Annual Report,* 1866.

[54] Quoted in Gill, "One Hundred Years Ago [—The Aeronautical Society]."

[55] T. O'B. Hubbard & J. L. Ledeboer, "Biographical Notice," in F. H. Wenham, *Aerial Locomotion* (see note 53), p. viii.

[56] "'Pharaoh's Bed,' Philae, from the Great Temple," *Egypt and Palestine,* II.

[57] Darrah, *World of Stereographs,* p. 4; Negretti and Zambra, London, *Negretti and Zambra Centenary 1850–1950* (London: Negretti and Zambra, 1950?), unpaged.

[58] Hubbard & Ledeboer, "Biographical Notice" (see notes 53 and 55), p. ix.

[59] *Photographic Journal,* III (May 21, 1857), pp. 275–76, and *Liverpool and Manchester Photographic Journal,* IV (May 15, 1857), p. 100, both reporting meeting of May 7, 1857.

[60] *Liverpool and Manchester Photographic Journal,* IV (Oct. 1, 1857), p. 206.

[61] For example, *Liverpool and Manchester Photographic Journal,* IV (June 1, 1857), p. 112.

[62] Letter in *Liverpool and Manchester Photographic Journal,* V (May 1, 1858), pp. 117–18.

[63] Negretti and Zambra, *Egypt and Nubia* appeared later and, in addition to describing the photographs, contained excerpts from reviews and other published comments.

[64] "Stereoscopic Views of Egypt," *Times*, London (Jan. 1, 1858), p. 9.

[65] *Photographic Notes*, III (Mar. 15, 1858), p. 73.

[66] *Athenaeum*, XXXI (Mar. 20, 1858), pp. 371–72.

[67] *Liverpool and Manchester Photographic Journal*, IV (Nov. 15, 1857), p. 244.

[68] S. Wilson, *Athenaeum*, XXXI (Apr. 10, 1858), p. 468.

[69] *Athenaeum*, XXXI (Apr. 17, 1858), p. 500.

[70] *Photographic Journal*, VIII (June 16, 1862), p. 75.

[71] "The Stereoscope," *British Journal of Photography*, XLV (Feb. 11, 1898), pp. 84–85; see also J. Van Haaften, "Francis Frith and Negretti & Zambra," *History of Photography*, IV (Jan. 1980), pp. 35–37 illus.

[72] "Manchester Mechanics' Institution: Photographic Dissolving Views," *Liverpool and Manchester Photographic Journal*, V (Jan. 15, 1858), p. 26; (Apr. 1, 1858), p. 82; (Apr. 15, 1858), p. 92.

[73] *Liverpool and Manchester Photographic Journal*, IV (Aug. 15, 1857), p. 167.

[74] IV (Nov. 15, 1857), p. 244.

[75] *Athenaeum*, XXXI (Feb. 20, 1858), p. 246.

[76] *Liverpool and Manchester Photographic Journal*, V (Mar. 1, 1858), p. 62.

[77] V (Apr. 1, 1858), p. 83; see also similar review in *Photographic Notes*, III (Mar. 1, 1858), p. 59.

[78] "The Photographic Exhibition," *Art Journal*, XX (Apr. 1, 1858), p. 121.

[79] *Liverpool and Manchester Photographic Journal*, IV (Dec. 1, 1857), p. 257.

[80] "Ramleh," *Egypt and Palestine*, II.

[81] There is reason, however, to be suspicious of this 1858 date: there are companion views for most of these 16-by-20-inch Pyramid photographs in the 7-by-9-inch format; and in all cases the companion views are numbered in a sequence that was used on the third and last trip in 1859–1860—a journey that took Frith back to the Holy Land via the "long desert" or overland route from Suez, down through Sinai and on to Gaza.

[82] "Absalom's Tomb, Jerusalem," *Egypt and Palestine*, II.

[83] "The Circular Temple, Baalbec," *Egypt and Palestine*, II.

[84] "View at Hebron," *Egypt and Palestine*, I.

[85] Negretti and Zambra, letter in *Photographic Notes*, III (Mar. 15, 1858), p. 76.

[86] "From Old Jewry to Jerusalem in One Night," *Athenaeum*, XXXI (June 19, 1858), p. 791; also *Notes and Queries*, 2nd Ser., VI (Oct. 2, 1858), p. 274.

[87] *Photographic Journal*, IV (June 21, 1858), p. 229.

[88] "Antiquities upon the Island of Biggeh, Near Philae," *Egypt and Palestine*, I.

[89] "'Pharaoh's Bed,' Island of Philae," *Egypt and Palestine*, I.

[90] "Portico of the Temple of Gerf Hossayn, Nubia," *Egypt and Palestine*, II.

[91] "Damascus," *Egypt, Sinai, and Palestine*.

[92] "Introduction," *Egypt and Palestine*, I.

[93] "'Pharaoh's Bed,' Island of Philae," *Egypt and Palestine*, I.

[94] "Granite Obelisk and Lotus Column, Karnac," *Egypt and Palestine*, I.

[95] "Damascus," *Egypt and Palestine*, I.

[96] "The Approach to Philae," *Egypt and Palestine*, II.

[97] *Photographic Journal*, IV (Mar. 22, 1858), p. 178.

[98] XX (Jan. 1, 1858), p. 30.

[99] "Egypt and Palestine," *Art Journal*, XX (Aug. 1, 1858), pp. 229–30.

[100] *Ibid.*

[101] "Photographic Contributions to Knowledge," *British Journal of Photography*, VII (Mar. 1, 1860), pp. 60–61.

[102] *Ibid.*

[103] See example bound in extra-illustrated copy of *Photographic News*, I (Nov. 12, 1858) in the collection of The New York Public Library.

[104] *Photographic Journal*, V (Mar. 5, 1859), p. 208.

[105] Interview with James Reilly, Rochester, N.Y., Mar. 6, 1979.

[106] *Photographic Journal*, V (Feb. 5, 1859), p. 179.

[107] *Athenaeum*, XXXIII (Jan. 8, 1859), p. 55.

[108] *British Journal of Photography*, VI (Feb. 1, 1859), p. 35.

[109] "Architectural Photographic Association," *Photographic News*, I (Jan. 7, 1859), pp. 207–08; also I (Dec. 24, 1858), p. 185; and *British Journal of Photography*, VI (Jan. 1, 1859), p. 7.

[110] *Athenaeum*, XXXII (Dec. 25, 1858), pp. 840–41; *Photographic Journal*, V (Dec. 11, 1858), p. 89.

[111] *Photographic Journal*, V (Jan. 21, 1859), pp. 145–48.

[112] *Notes and Queries*, 2nd Ser., VII (Jan. 15, 1859), p. 60.

[113] "Birmingham Photographic Society," *British Journal of Photography*, VI (Jan. 15, 1859), p. 21.

[114] *Art Journal*, XXI (Mar. 1, 1859), pp. 71–72.

[115] *Photographic News*, I (Jan. 7, 1859), p. 208.

[116] "Philae from the South," *Upper Egypt and Ethiopia*.

[117] Hoskins, *A Winter in Upper and Lower Egypt*, pp. 105–06.

[118] "Exhibition: Architectural Photographic Association," *British Journal of Photography*, VIII (Feb. 1, 1861), p. 51.

[119] "The Temple of Soleb, Ethiopia," *Upper Egypt and Ethiopia*.

[120] "Ruins of the Temple of Amara, Ethiopia," *Upper Egypt and Ethiopia*.

[121] *Photographic News*, III (Feb. 10, 1860), p. 279.

[122] *Ibid.*

[123] "Osiride Pillar at Medinet-Haboo," *Lower Egypt, Thebes, and the Pyramids*.

[124] "View in the Interior of the Hall of Columns, Karnac," *Lower Egypt, Thebes, and the Pyramids*.

[125] Jay, *Victorian Cameraman*, p. 19.

[126] *Photographic Notes*, III (Nov. 4, 1859), p. 99.

[127] *British Journal of Photography*, VII (May 1, 1860), p. 136.

[128] "Frith's Photographs of Egypt and Palestine, and the Collection of Egyptian Products at the Crystal Palace," *Art Journal*, XXII (Nov. 1, 1860), pp. 348–49.

[129] "Architectural Photographic Association," *Photographic Journal*, VII (Oct. 15, 1861), p. 295.

[130] "Fine Arts: Architectural Photographic Association," *Athenaeum*, XXXVII (Jan. 26, 1861), p. 124; also *Photographic News*, V (Jan. 18, 1861), p. 26, (Jan. 25, 1861), p. 37; and *British Journal of Photography*, VIII (Feb. 1, 1861), pp. 50–51.

[131] *Athenaeum*, XL (Oct. 18, 1862), p. 504.

[132] Jay, p. 21.

[133] It is possible that Frith's companion on his last and sentimental journey to Egypt was Mary Ann's older brother William. Family documents show that he remained in Cairo and died there in December 1860. See Jay, p. 28.

[134] "Notes Literary and Photographic," *Photographic Journal*, VII (Jan. 15, 1862), p. 360; see also Gill, "One Hundred Years Ago [—Frith's Bible]."

[135] "Notes Literary and Photographic," (see preceding note).

[136] "Notes Literary and Photographic," *Photographic Journal*, VII (Feb. 15, 1862), p. 378, introducing a quote from *The Critic*.

[137] *Photographic News*, V (Jan. 25, 1861), p. 37.

[138] S. Sharpe, "Preface," in F. Frith, *Egypt, Nubia, and Ethiopia*.

[139] *British Journal of Photography*, IX (Aug. 1, 1862), p. 290.

[140] *Photographic Journal*, VII (Feb. 15, 1862), p. 378.

[141] *Ibid.*; see also *Athenaeum*, XXXIX (Feb. 15, 1862), p. 157.

[142] Quoted in *Photographic News*, VI (July 25, 1862), p. 355.

[143] *Art Journal*, N.S., I (Mar. 1, 1862), p. 96.

[144] *Photographic Journal*, VII (July 15, 1862), p. 80.

[145] This garment is still in the Frith family. See Jay, p. 33.

[146] *British Journal of Photography*, XLV (Mar. 4, 1898), p. 141; (Mar. 11, 1898), p. 158.

[147] *British Journal of Photography*, XLV (Feb. 11, 1898), pp. 84–85.

[148] Jay, p. 7.

[149] "Photography: The Francis Frith Collection," *ARTnewsletter*, III (Nov. 1, 1977), p. 5.

BIBLIOGRAPHY

CHRONOLOGICAL LIST OF BOOKS CONTAINING ORIGINAL PHOTOGRAPHS BY FRANCIS FRITH

Egypt and Palestine Photographed and Described by Francis Frith (London: J. S. Virtue [1858–1860]). 2 vols. Issued in 25 parts; 76 albumen prints, approx. 8¾ × 6½ inches / 225 × 165 mm.

Cairo, Sinai, Jerusalem, and the Pyramids of Egypt; A Series of Sixty Photographic Views by Francis Frith. With Descriptions by Mrs. Poole and Reginald Stuart Poole (London: J. S. Virtue [1860, 1861?]). Issued in 20 parts; 60 albumen prints, approx. 8¾ × 6½ inches / 225 × 165 mm.

Egypt, Sinai, and Jerusalem; A Series of Twenty Photographic Views by Francis Frith. With Descriptions by Mrs. Poole and Reginald Stuart Poole (London: W. Mackenzie [1860?]). 20 albumen prints, approx. 15 × 19 inches / 380 × 480 mm.
Republished: (London: J. S. Virtue [1862]). Issued in 10 parts.

The Holy Bible . . . ; Illustrated with Photographic Views of Biblical Scenery from Nature by Frith (London: J. E. Eyre & W. Spottiswoode, 1862). 20 albumen prints, approx. 8¾ × 6½ inches / 225 × 165 mm.

Egypt, Nubia, and Ethiopia; Illustrated by One Hundred Stereoscopic Photographs, Taken by Francis Frith for Messrs. Negretti and Zambra. With Descriptions and Numerous Wood Engravings, by Joseph Bonomi . . . and Notes by Samuel Sharpe. (London: Smith, Elder & Co., 1862). 100 albumen stereo pairs.

The Holy Bible; Containing the Old and New Testaments . . . Illustrated with Photographs by Frith (Glasgow: W. Mackenzie, 1862–1863). Second title page: *The Queen's Bible.* 56 albumen prints, approx. 8¾ × 6½ inches / 225 × 165 mm.

Sinai and Palestine.
Lower Egypt, Thebes, and the Pyramids.
Upper Egypt and Ethiopia.
Egypt, Sinai, and Palestine, Supplementary Volume. (London: W. Mackenzie [1862?]). Four-volume series; each volume contains 36 albumen prints, approx. 8¾ × 6½ inches / 225 × 165 mm., and 1 smaller, cropped albumen print mounted on first title page; total of 148 albumen prints; text by Frith.

OTHER WORKS CONSULTED OR CITED

Arago, Dominique-François, "Le Daguerréotype," *Comptes rendus des séances de l'Académie des Sciences,* IX (19 août 1839), pp. 250–67.

Brewster, Sir David, *The Stereoscope; Its History, Theory and Construction with its Application to the Fine and Applied Arts and to Education* (London: John Murray, 1856).

Brockedon, William, *Egypt and Nubia; From Drawings Made on the Spot by David Roberts, R.A.* (London: F. G. Moon, 1846–1849). 3 vols.

Brugsch, Heinrich Karl, *Reiseberichte aus Aegypten* (Leipzig: F. A. Brockhaus, 1855).

Bull, Deborah, and Donald Lorimor, *Up the Nile; A Photographic Excursion: Egypt 1839–1898* (N.Y.: Clarkson N. Potter [1979]).

Cameron, Donald Andreas, *Egypt in the Nineteenth Century; or, Mehemet Ali and His Successors Until the British Occupation in 1882* (London: Smith, Elder, 1898).

Comparative Photography; A Century of Change in Egypt and Israel. Photographs by Francis Frith & Jane Reese Williams. Introduction by Brian M. Fagan. "Untitled No. 17" ([Carmel, Calif.]: Friends of Photography [1979]).

Cramb, John, *Jerusalem in 1860: A Series of Photographic Views, Taken . . . by J. Cramb . . . With Descriptive Letterpress by the Rev. Robert Buchanan* (Glasgow: William Collins, 1860).

Croly, George, *The Holy Land, Syria, Idumea, Arabia, Egypt & Nubia from Drawings Made on the Spot by David Roberts, R.A.* (London: F. G. Moon, 1842–1844?). 3 vols.
2nd. ed. (London: Day & Son, 1855–1856). 6 vols.; includes text by William Brockedon.

Darrah, William Culp, *Stereo Views; A History of Stereographs in America and Their Collection* (Gettysburg: Times and News Pub. Co., 1964).

——, *The World of Stereographs* (Gettysburg: Darrah, 1977).

Dawson, Warren R., and Eric P. Uphill, *Who Was Who in Egyptology,* 2nd ed. (London: Egypt Exploration Society, 1972).

De Leon, Edwin, *The Khedives' Egypt; or, The Old House of Bondage under New Masters* (N.Y.: Harper's, 1878).

DuCamp, Maxime, *Égypte, Nubie, Palestine et Syrie; Dessins photographiques recueillis pendant les années 1849, 1850 et 1851 accompagnés d'un texte explicatif* (Paris: Gide et J. Baudry, 1852).

Flaubert, Gustave, *Flaubert in Egypt: A Sensibility on Tour; A Narrative Drawn from Gustave Flaubert's Travel Notes & Letters,* translated from the French and edited by Francis Steegmuller (London: Bodley Head, 1972).

Frith, Francis, "The Art of Photography," *The Art Journal,* XXI (March 1, 1859), pp. 71–72.

Gernsheim, Helmut and Alison, *The History of Photography; From the Camera Obscura to the Beginning of the Modern Era* (N.Y.: McGraw-Hill, 1969).

Gill, Arthur T., "One Hundred Years Ago [—The Aeronautical Society]," *The Photographic Journal,* CVI (Oct. 1966), p. 354.

——, "One Hundred Years Ago [—Frith's Bible]," *The Photographic Journal,* CII (Jan. 1962), p. 39.

Girault de Prangey, Joseph-Philibert, *Monuments arabes d'Égypte, de Syrie, et d'Asie mineure; dessinés et mesurés de 1842 à 1845* (Paris [1846]). 6 parts.

Good, George, *The History of the Liverpool Amateur Photographic Association from 1853 to 1953* (Liverpool: L.A.P.A., 1953).

Greene, J. B., *Le Nil* ([Paris?] 1854).

Hardwich, T. Frederick, *A Manual of Photographic Chemistry; Including the Practice of the Collodion Process*, 3rd ed. (London: Churchill, 1856).

———, "Reminiscences of Twenty Years Ago," *Anthony's Photographic Bulletin*, VI (April 1875), p. 99.

Hemphill, Chris, "Frith's Photographic Views of Egypt," *Nineteenth Century*, III (Summer 1977), pp. 70–73.

Horeau, Hector, *Panorama d'Égypte et de Nubie . . .* (Paris, 1841).

Hoskins, George Alexander, *Travels in Ethiopia; Above the Second Cataract of the Nile* (London: Longman, Rees, Orme, Brown, Green, & Longman, 1835).

———, *A Winter in Upper and Lower Egypt* (London: Hurst and Blackett, 1863).

Jammes, André and Marie-Thérèse, "Egypt in Flaubert's Time: An Exhibition of the First Photographers, 1839–1860," *Aperture*, No. 78 (1977), pp. 62–77.

Jay, Bill, *Victorian Cameraman; Francis Frith's Views of Rural England 1850–1898* (Newton Abbot: David & Charles, 1973).

Jenson, Dale A., and Caroline P. Wister, "The Big Picture; Photographic Images From the 19th Century: Catalogue," *Nineteenth Century*, IV (Spring 1978), p. 112, item 42.

Jullian, Philippe, *The Orientalists: European Painters of Eastern Scenes* (Oxford: Phaidon [1977]).

Keith, Alexander, *Evidence of the Truth of the Christian Religion*, 36th ed. (Edinburgh: W. Whyte, 1848).

37th ed., much enlarged, with daguerreotype views (London, Edinburgh . . .: T. Nelson, 1859).

Kinglake, Alexander William, *Eōthen; or, Traces of Travel Brought Home from the East . . .* (London: J. Ollivier, 1844).

Leroux, Charles, "Kindlers of Ancient Love Affairs with Light; the Rare Art of Albumen Paper-Making and Printing Is Restored," *American Photographer*, I (Nov. 1978), pp. 72–79.

London. International Exhibition, 1862, *Catalogue of Photographs Exhibited in Class XIV* (London: Trounce, 1862).

Ma'oz, Moshe, ed. *Studies on Palestine During the Ottoman Period* (Jerusalem: Magnes Press, Hebrew University and Yad Izhak Ben-Zvi, 1975).

Marlowe, John, *Spoiling the Egyptians* (London: Andre Deutsch, 1974).

Nassau, William E., "Treasures on Glass and Celluloid: Conservation Work of the Photographic Archives of the Palestine Exploration Fund," *Palestine Exploration Quarterly*, CX (July–Dec. 1978), pp. 131–33.

Negretti and Zambra, *Egypt and the Holy Land. Descriptive Catalogue of a Second Series of Views in Egypt and the Holy Land, from Negatives by F. Frith, Esq. . . .* (London [ca. 1859–1861]).

———, *Egypt and Nubia: Descriptive Catalogue of One Hundred Stereoscopic Views of the Pyramids, the Nile, Karnak, Thebes,*

Aboo-Simbel and All the Most Interesting Objects of Egypt and Nubia (London [1857–1858]).

"News and Notes," *Palestine Exploration Quarterly*, CX (July–Dec. 1978), pp. 73–74.

Palgrave, William Gifford, "A Visit to Upper Egypt in the Hot Season," *Macmillan's Magazine*, XV (Jan. 1867), pp. 247–56.

"Photography: The Francis Frith Collection," *ARTnewsletter*, III (Nov. 1, 1977), p. 5.

Robinson, Edward, *Biblical Researches in Palestine and the Adjacent Regions: A Journal of Travels in the Years 1838 & 1852*, 2nd ed. (London: J. Murray, 1856). 3 vols.

Salzmann, Auguste, *Jérusalem; étude et reproduction photographique des monuments de la Ville Sainte, depuis l'époque judaïque jusqu'à nos jours* (Paris: Gide et J. Baudry, 1856).

Searight, Sara, *The British in the Middle East* (London: Weidenfeld and Nicolson, 1964).

Stanley, Arthur Penrhyn, *Sinai and Palestine in Connection with Their History* (London: Murray, 1856).

New ed. (London: Murray, 1862).

Teynard, Félix, *Égypte et Nubie; sites et monuments les plus intéressants pour l'étude de l'art de l'histoire* (Paris, N.Y., etc.: Goupil, 1858). 2 vols.

Thackeray, William Makepeace, *Notes of a Journey From Cornhill to Grand Cairo; by Way of Lisbon, Athens, Constantinople, and Jerusalem: Performed in the Steamers of the Peninsular and Oriental Company* (London: Chapman and Hall, 1846).

Thompson, W. M., *The Holy Land, Egypt, Constantinople, Athens, . . .; A Series of Forty-eight Photographs, Taken by F. Bedford, for . . . the Prince of Wales During the Tour in the East . . .* (London, 1866).

Thornthwaite, William Henry, *A Guide to Photography, Containing Simple and Concise Directions for Obtaining Views, . . .* 9th–16th ed. (London: Simpkin, Marshall, Horne and Thornthwaite, 1855–1858).

Tibawi, A. L. *British Interests in Palestine 1800–1901* (Toronto: Oxford University Press, 1961).

Watson, Sir C. M., *Palestine Exploration Fund; Fifty Years' Work in the Holy Land; A Record and a Summary 1865–1915* (London: Committee of the Palestine Exploration Fund, 1915).

Welling, William, *Photography in America; The Formative Years 1839–1900* (N.Y.: Crowell, 1978).

Wilkinson, Sir John Gardner, *The Architecture of Ancient Egypt* (London: J. Murray, 1850).

———, *Modern Egypt and Thebes* (London: J. Murray, 1843). 2 vols.

Published in a condensed form as: *Murray's Handbook for Travellers in Egypt; . . . the Course of the Nile, . . . the Peninsula of Mount Sinai, . . .* (London: J. Murray, 1847; new ed., 1858).

Wilson, Charles W., *Ordnance Survey of Jerusalem; Made with the Sanction of the Earl de Grey and Ripon, . . .* (London, 1865).

Wortham, J. D. *The Genesis of British Egyptology 1549–1906* (Norman: University of Oklahoma Press, 1971).

FOREWORD TO THE PLATES
by Jon E. Manchip White

Each of the four volumes in the Mackenzie edition of ca. 1862 contains exactly 37 Near Eastern Plates by Francis Frith, making a total of 148. Of these, I have selected 77, attempting to weed out the photographs that by modern standards lack adequate clarity and definition, or that in subject and content merely duplicate others. I have tried to choose those which are pictorially striking and which also shed a piquant light on the archaeological or cultural conditions of the Near East in the middle of the nineteenth century. I have also rearranged the photographs in a more coherent and logical sequence than they possess in the original volumes, where they are arranged in a somewhat haphazard fashion. Thus I have started with three photographs that are practically the only nonantiquarian images in Frith's collection, in order to set the tone, and have marshalled the remainder strictly in the order: Egypt (Plates 4–45), Nubia (parts of modern Egypt and Sudan, Plates 46–54), Sinai (Plates 55–59), Palestine (sites now in Israel, Plates 60–72),* Lebanon (Baalbek, Plates 73 & 74) and Syria (Damascus, Plates 75–77). The book now seems to possess, particularly in a single volume, a more clear and simple narrative flow.

In this, the world's first methodically planned and executed photographic safari (accomplished in three separate trips), Frith offers us a comprehensive view of what the great historical monuments of the Near East looked like in his own time. It is interesting to compare these sites with how they appear today. Frith shows us many temples, palaces, towns and pyramids in an untouched and romantically ruinous state; some were in the early stages of being disinterred and tidied up through the heroic exertions of the first generation of modern archaeologists; and some have degenerated further or have totally disappeared from the face of the earth. It is a fascinating record.

A minor point, about Egypt. In that country, which constitutes the bulk of his work, Frith made no photographs to the north of Cairo. Thus there are no pictures of sites in the Nile Delta—and in fact there were really, in that steamy and waterlogged terrain, no significant monuments for him to photograph, as there are precious few today. Nevertheless,

the Delta below Cairo once constituted the kingdom of Lower Egypt, which was of equal if not on occasion of more importance than the kingdom of Upper Egypt, south of Cairo, in which Frith took his photographs. The great cities of the Delta did not survive: so when we look at Frith's pictures we should bear in mind that we are looking at only half of the historical story, only half of what ancient Egypt actually was.

Frith accompanied each of his photographs with a substantial "article," a page or two of commentary. For our modern taste, the tone of these mid-Victorian commentaries is perhaps a shade too pompous and ornate, the humor a trifle heavy-handed. Frith confined his "articles" almost entirely to discussions of the antiquarian aspects of his pictures, and much of his material (though by no means all) has been superseded by later scholarship. However, I have tried to retain the more personal and amusing sidelights from his commentaries in order to enliven and add contrast to my own historical notes.

From these random remarks, we gather, among other things, that Frith was extremely well educated and well read, in all ways fitted for his exacting travels. It is also clear that he was a deeply sensitive, perhaps in some ways an oversensitive man (his self-portrait, Plate I, is revealing in this respect) who found several aspects of his Near Eastern journeys distinctly trying to his nerves. He was no Sir Richard Burton. He hated the dirt, the dust, the flies, the squalor of Arab towns. He disliked the behavior of the cheeky and irrepressible Arab children—so different from the behavior of the well-brought-up children of Victorian England. He found Arab habitations dreary and disgusting, avoiding them whenever he could and preferring the clean air and elbow room of the Nile or the desert, whatever their hardships. We can guess that his raw nerves and exasperation were underscored by the difficulties of transporting and operating his large, heavy cameras and attending to his precious stock of collodion plates in such surroundings. His occasional irritations can be readily understood and forgiven, and in any case they make him appear very human.

By any standards, his achievement was remarkable and admirable. Long forgotten, it is a distinct pleasure to bring it back to the attention of a new generation of readers and students.

* [As mentioned in the Introduction, throughout this book "Palestine" is used in its ancient geographical sense, with no reference to its special meaning in contemporary politics.—PUBLISHER]

THE PLATES

1   FRITH IN TURKISH COSTUME

What the well-dressed visitor to the Near East wore on his travels. The Victorians had a mania for wearing "native costume"—provided it was sufficiently picturesque and belonged to the upper rather than the lower class of the country in question.

In fact Frith would have worn such a costume during a large part of his travels, though not when he was in major cities like Cairo or Jerusalem, where a sizeable influx of Europeans was already roaming the streets, seeing the sights and staying in the Western-style hostelries that were springing up in the late 1840s and 1850s.

Frith is shown wearing Turkish costume because the Turks were at that time the overlords of the entire area in which he would be traveling. A vast region as far as the Persian Gulf, throughout Arabia, Palestine, Egypt and the whole of North Africa (except for Algeria, recently taken over by the French), was subject to the Sultan in Constantinople. Moreover, in spite of the fact that it was "the sick man of Europe," and despite the brutal nature of many of its policies that made its allies

shudder, the Ottoman Empire was supported by England and France. This was because it was a buffer against the determined attempts of Russia to break out of the Black Sea and into the Mediterranean, and to penetrate the Near East and the Indian subcontinent. In 1855 Turkey had joined the British and the French in invading the Crimea, thereby cementing the alliance.

Egypt enjoyed a special status within the Ottoman Empire. Its ruling dynasty paid nominal lip service to the Sublime Porte, but had been made virtually independent by Mohammed Ali and his gifted son Ibrahim Pasha, who at one time threatened to attack and capture Constantinople itself and was only restrained by the intervention of Britain and France. In Egypt, then, Frith was technically on Turkish soil. However, the British presence was already making itself felt with ever-increasing weight, and a little over 20 years later, in the early 1880s, Britain would take the country formally under its wing.

2 FRITH'S BOAT ON THE NILE

Many Englishmen made the Grand Tour as casual tourists in circumstances of passable comfort; not many made it with the professional dedication and determined spirit of Francis Frith. Frith's travels entailed negotiating a thousand miles of river, desert and mountain, from Sudan to Syria, and took him right away from the well-beaten tourist tracks. Part of his traveling was done on horseback, part by camel, part on a Nile boat such as the one in the photograph. None of these conveyances was comfortable.

Frith's little ark, which housed himself, his dragoman, a couple of servants and the crew, seems even smaller than the very similar boats in which the great American Orientalist James Henry Breasted made his epic epigraphical voyages from 1905 onward. Any reader who wishes to obtain a graphic idea of what Nile travel entailed in the past should read that minor masterpiece, *Pioneer to the Past*, Charles Breasted's beautifully executed biography of his father.

Like Frith, Breasted used convenient tombs as his darkroom, working by candlelight, and the practice became standard in Egyptological photography. Harry Burton, the brilliant photographer who worked with Carter on the tomb of Tutankhamon, also converted for his use a dry, commodious, empty and handy tomb, as described in Howard Carter's and A. C. Mace's *The Discovery of the Tomb of Tutankhamen* (1923; Dover reprint, 1977).

3 ARAB SPORTSMAN AND COOK

One cannot do better than quote some of Frith's comments on this plate. They cast an entertaining light on Frith's travels and on his own character and attitudes.

"The group before us," he writes, "is one with which every traveller in the East will claim acquaintance, recognising at once the man of many resources, who has never failed to produce a dinner, and the scarcely less useful purveyor, who so often has brought the wished-for material at a culinary crisis. . . .

"[Arab sportsmen] rarely, indeed try a distant, still less a flying shot, but it must be recollected that the general weapon is an ancestor of our much-regretted Brown Bess, and that powder is expensive. Their performances, however, are accompanied with observations that add very much to their interest. If successful, they warmly congratulate themselves; if unlucky, they heap the most extraordinary maledictions upon the intended prize, its ancestors and connections. The favourite bird is the kata or sand-grouse, but the desert also affords red-legged partridges, and, in the neighbourhood of the Red Sea, various kinds of wild fowl.

"The Arab cook, when the study of the European digestion and temper has taught him to be moderate with butter and oil, is a true genius. . . . Where not a trace of meat, alive or dead, has been seen, a succession of savoury dishes appear as though by magic. What is most wonderful is, that this great engineer is a man of scruples; his chief charm, if he be a Muslim, is his religious cleanliness, and, therefore, the anxious mind is not troubled with visions of forbidden meat: the leg of a donkey is impossible, a dog is unheard of . . . . We should advise any traveller who would make the journey up the Nile and through Sinai and Palestine in comfort, to secure, instead of a dragoman, a good cook, who could speak a little English or Italian."

4 CAIRO: TOMBS IN THE SOUTHERN CEMETERY

The buildings in the foreground are part of the Karafa, or southern cemetery, one of the two great Cairene cemeteries dating from the time of the early Arab conquest of Egypt (640 A.D.). Its tomb-mosques and chapels housed the bones of Cairo's first Arab rulers, soldiers, poets and holy men, including that of the Prophet's own standard-bearer. However, we must remember that the history of Cairo, situated as it is at the strategic point where the Nile meets the Delta, marking off Upper from Lower Egypt, traditionally extended backward in time for some 4000 years before Caliph Omar's general Amr occupied the city. The ancient Egyptians believed that the venerable city of Memphis, situated 17 miles south of modern Cairo, had been founded by the shadowy Menes, Egypt's first pharaoh and the unifier of the Two Lands. Close by, a short distance to the northeast, lay the almost equally ancient religious city of On, or Heliopolis, today a Cairo suburb.

Beyond the buildings of the Karafa, most of which were endowed in

their heyday as hospitals and shelters for travelers and for the needy, can be seen the stout walls of the Citadel. The Citadel was begun by the great Sultan Saladin, who passed eight years of his 24-year reign in Cairo, and was built with the labor of the thousands of Christian slaves captured in the Crusades. Work started in 1176 or 1177 and was completed in 1207–1208 in the reign of his nephew and successor, the Sultan el-Kamil.

Dominating the skyline is the enormous mosque of Mohammed Ali, which in spite of its prominence and celebrity is not as venerable as many of its visitors suppose. It was begun by Mohammed Ali, the Lion of the Levant, an Albanian mercenary who established a virtually independent dynasty in 1805 and with whom the history of modern Egypt begins. He began the mosque in 1824, and when Frith took his photograph in 1856 it had still not received its finishing touches.

5 CAIRO: THE BAB EL-AZAB GATEWAY AT THE CITADEL

Until 1850, the Citadel was the residence of the rulers of Cairo, many of whom, from the time of Saladin onward, were to leave their mark on it. It was a rabbit warren of fortifications, battlements and passageways, and the Bab el-Azab commanded the entrance to one of its three principal *enceintes*. Named for his Azabs, or corps of Turkish mercenaries, it was built by the eighteenth-century Mameluke Ridwan el-Gelfi, a humane and tolerant ruler who liked to enjoy a relaxed and cultivated existence at his pleasure dome on the Lake of Ezbekiya, two miles northwest of the Citadel. His reign is remembered as a golden interlude in the generally bloody history of the Mamelukes in Egypt, and he deserved a better fate than to be shot by conspirators while having his head shaved.

It was behind the Bab el-Azab, restored since Frith photographed it to its original condition, that there took place the famous massacre of the Mamelukes at the hands of Mohammed Ali on March 1, 1811.

Mohammed Ali, after securing the patronage of the Turkish suzerains of Egypt, realized that he could never rule secure and supreme until he had broken the power of the Mamelukes, the military barons, descendants of Saladin's officers, who had until that time owned the estates and wielded the principal influence in Egypt. Accordingly, he called 500 of their leaders to a grand reception and review at the Citadel. As they were riding down the slope and between the steep walls toward the Bab el-Azab, which gives onto the ancient Roumaliya Square (where Frith set up his camera), on a prearranged signal the gates at each end of the passage were slammed shut. Then a merciless fusillade was poured down from the walls above into the mass of gorgeously caparisoned men and horses trapped and churning about helplessly in the narrow confines below until every sign of life was extinct. Such a man was Mohammed Ali, and with his slaughter of the Mamelukes medieval Egypt, with all its color, and all its crimes and glories, came to an end.

6 CAIRO: THE MOSQUE OF THE CALIPH EL-HAKIM

Frith made a special study of only a half-dozen of the principal mosques of Cairo, whereas the modern visitor fails in his duty unless he attempts to see at least a score of the outstanding examples. No doubt he found it difficult, in the teeming environs of Cairo, to hit upon a tranquil moment when his picture would not be spoiled by worshippers or casual pedestrians. It also must have required a large expenditure of *baksheesh* to persuade the people whom he kept in his pictures, for the sake of scale and local color, to stand or sit still.

The mosque of the Fatimid Caliph Hakim was built between 990 and 1003, but fell into the ruin in which Frith depicts it as early as the 1450s. The Crusaders had the temerity to build a Christian church inside it which functioned until Saladin pulled it down. After it became disused as a religious building, the mosque became successively a lamp factory, a rope works, and now, more happily, an elementary school.

Its checkered history and gloomy atmosphere reflect the personality of its founder. It was established to honor the insane pretensions of the Caliph Hakim, who styled himself the Soul of Adam and the Creator of the Universe. He was the initiator of the fanatical sect of the Druzes. His conduct made the antics of the most bizarre Egyptian autocrat of our own day, King Farouk, seem pallid and amiable by comparison. Among other things, Hakim ordered all the vines in Cairo to be cut down, all the dogs to be killed, and all the honey and similar luxuries to be thrown into the Nile. He decreed that the Cairenes must sleep by day and work by night, and for the last seven years of his reign no woman was allowed to leave her house and set foot in the street. The penalty for the slightest misbehavior was instant disemboweling or beheading. Not surprisingly he was not lamented, except by the Druzes, when his reign of terror came to an end with his mysterious disappearance in 1021.

7 Cairo: the Mosque of the Sultan Quait Bey

The tomb-mosque of the Circassian Mameluke the Sultan Quait Bey has been admired ever since its completion in 1742 as a well-nigh perfect example of Cairene architecture. Nowhere else can be seen such a subtle, happy harmony of dome, minaret, octagon, circle, square, oblong and triangle.

Quait Bey scattered mosques, caravanserais, colleges and palaces with a liberal hand throughout the Near East. He was a great traveler, visiting Syria, Mesopotamia and the farthest reaches of Egypt, and he made pilgrimages to Jerusalem and to Mecca. This cultured man began life as a slave, was sold by one sultan to another, and advanced steadily through nine brief and bloodsoaked reigns to the seat of power. He ruled for no less than 29 years and died in his bed—an achievement that can be measured by the fact that the other 25 rulers of the

Circassian dynasty averaged reigns of less than six years apiece. However, in spite of his taste for the civilized elements of life, he could match his less sophisticated predecessors in the uncertainty of his temper. He was known to thrash his viziers with his own hands and was a formidable putter-out-of-eyes and tearer-out-of-tongues. He tortured and put to death the celebrated scientist Ali Ibn el-Marshushi for failing to turn lead into gold.

The interior of the mosque, which stands in the cemetery named after Quait Bey on the northeast side of the Citadel, is a marvel of carved stone, plaster, mosaic and colored glass, offering a superb display of arabesque and geometrical decoration. It is a pity that Frith's apparatus and the religious prejudices of the time prevented him from photographing the inside of this and other religious buildings.

8 CAIRO: EZBEKIYA

Here is the heart of Cairo as it existed over a century ago. Named after a revered emir, Ezbek Ibn Tushtush, the Ezbekiya represented the northern artery of the city. Here stood the great houses of the princes and the leading merchants. Here the rulers of the land took their ease beside its lake and on the borders of its famous canal. Here Napoleon and other foreign conquerors took up their residence. It was on a terrace of the French headquarters overlooking the Ezbekiya that General Kléber, Napoleon's viceroy, was stabbed to death in 1800; and less than 50 years before Frith took this photograph the thoroughfare had been lined with poles on which were stuck the severed heads of 450 of the British soldiers whom Mohammed Ali captured when he beat back the attempt of General Frazer to invade Egypt in 1807. (One of these captives, a Scottish private soldier called Keith, turned Moslem and proved such a faithful champion of Islam that he eventually became the governor of the holy city of Medina.)

In the Ezbekiya rose many of the more august hotels of the Victorian era that were built to accommodate the flood of foreign tourists and residents who arrived in Egypt in the 1850s. Here stood Shepheard's, where Frith himself stayed, until it was burned out on Black Saturday, January 26, 1952, when most of European Cairo was put to the torch. Nearby was the Turf Club, which together with the Sporting Club at Gezira was one of the bastions of British social life in Cairo, and which also went up in flames on Black Saturday. In the Ezbekiya Gardens was situated the charming little white wooden opera house inaugurated by the Khedive Ismail in 1869. For its first production Verdi had been commissioned to write *Aïda*, to mark the opening of the Suez Canal in that same year; but the production could not be made ready in time and *Rigoletto* had to be put on instead. Sadly, the pretty little opera house, a touch of Paris in the center of Cairo, was burned down in its turn—though accidentally—a few years ago.

9 THE STEP PYRAMID AT SAKKARA

"The day and hour in a man's life when he first obtains a view of 'The Pyramids,'" runs Frith's commentary on a related plate (our No. 12), "is a time to date from for many a year to come; he is approaching, as it were, the presence of an immortality which has mingled vaguely with his thoughts from very childhood, and has been to him unconsciously an essential and beautiful *form*, and the most majestic mystery ever created by man." These words are surely as true today as they were then, though a corner of the mystery has been lifted a little.

The sad state of the Step Pyramid at the time when Frith set eyes upon it can be judged from his photograph. Today, many of the elegant and sophisticated buildings in the mortuary complex surrounding the pyramid with its four six-stepped sides have been splendidly restored. The complex included buildings designed to celebrate the royal coronation and jubilee, in addition to the royal mortuary chapel. The buildings were decorated with exquisite carving and tiling, and were surrounded by an elaborately recessed wall, a mile long and 33 feet high, buttressed with bastions and supplied with 14 gateways, 13 of them dummies.

The Step Pyramid, built for the wise king Zoser of the Third Dynasty, who ruled about 2800–2700 B.C., was the inspiration of his vizier or chief minister, Imhotep, whose fame was to outshine that of his master. Imhotep was an authentic genius, an ancient Egyptian Leonardo da Vinci, who not only created the world's first truly substantial building in stone, the Step Pyramid, but was also a sage and scientist who was subsequently deified as the god of medicine (the origin of the Greek god Aesculapius). Two thousand years after Imhotep's death, the sick and the lame were still making pilgrimages to his shrine at Sakkara.

The pyramid that appears in the foreground was begun by Zoser, but remained unfinished at his death and was never completed.

10   THE PYRAMIDS AT DAHSHUR

It appears likely that the Step Pyramid at Sakkara was followed in sequence by a stepped pyramid built for Huny, a shadowy monarch who followed Zoser and whose reign closed the Third Dynasty. Huny did not live to see his monument completed, and it was promptly appropriated by Sneferu, the first pharaoh of the mighty Fourth Dynasty. It was Sneferu, who acceded to the throne about 2615 B.C., who certainly erected the Southern or Bent Pyramid at Dahshur and its companion the Northern Pyramid, a mile away across the plain.

It has been possible to compute, from the dilapidated remnant of the Northern Pyramid (nearer the camera), that it was in fact the first true pyramid, its sides an uninterrupted slope ascending at an angle of approximately 45 degrees rather than the steeper 52 degrees of later examples. As for the Bent Pyramid nearby, its lower courses rise at an angle of 52 degrees before changing abruptly to one of 42 degrees. The reason for the change in angle is unknown. It may be that the design of the pyramid was deliberate, as the general pyramid concept was still in an early and fluid stage; or it may be that, with his death approaching, Sneferu found himself running out of time and did not want his monument to suffer the same fate as Zoser's second pyramid, or Huny's; alternatively, his successor might have piously but speedily finished it off for him. We should note that the Bent Pyramid is in an excellent and unusual state of preservation, with much of its original coat of limestone still intact.

Probably at least three overlapping and associated ideas came into the mind of an ancient Egyptian when he looked at a pyramid. First, there was the notion expressed in a Fifth Dynasty text: "A staircase is laid for Pharaoh, that he may ascend to heaven thereby." Second, the angle of the sides would have reminded him of the angle assumed by the rays of the sacred sun as it struck through the heavens and enfolded the earth. Third, the gilded triangular capstone at the summit of every pyramid was symbolic of the *benben* or holy "Hillock of Eternity" on which the creator god Ra-Atum had first made his appearance.

11   THE PYRAMIDS OF GIZA

Frith's general view of the majestic assemblage of pyramids was taken from the point at which modern practitioners customarily set up their cameras—which testifies to the keen eye of this pioneer of the art with his much more cumbersome equipment. The appearance of the Giza pyramids, seen at ground level and from this vantage point, is not greatly altered today.

The pyramids were built, in order from the right and in order of size, by Khufu (Greek version, Kheops or Cheops), Khafra (Khephren or Chephren) and Menkaure (Mycerinus), respectively the second, third and fourth pharaohs of the Fourth Dynasty. They ruled between 2600 and 2500 B.C. The middle pyramid, Khafra's, looks taller than Khufu's, but this is merely an illusion due to the fact that its sides are steeper and it stands at a slightly higher elevation on the plateau. The three miniature pyramids at the left are those of Menkaure's queens; a similar trio of small pyramids was built by Khufu for his own queens, and are just out of sight beyond the right-hand edge of the picture. Originally the entire area around the pyramids was seamed and dotted with temples, tomb shafts, roads, causeways, pits for sacred boats, and the *mastabas* or squat one-story tombs of favored courtiers.

The buildings attached to Mycerinus' pyramid were completed and remained long in use, but the pyramid itself was never finished. It is possible that this indicates that the practice of pyramid building waned with the last years of the dynasty—and indeed may have hastened its end, in view of the prodigious outpouring of effort and treasure that it must have entailed. However, pyramid building did not come to a complete halt and carried over in a modified form into the Fifth and Sixth Dynasties, and was substantially revived as late as the Twelfth. But in conception and construction these later pyramids were much humbler, and utilized less permanent materials. They disintegrated into inchoate heaps of rubble, and although they were close to Sakkara there was no reason why Frith's attention should have been drawn to them.

12 THE GREAT PYRAMID AND THE SPHINX

The sand had been cleared from around the Sphinx on several occasions in the earlier part of the nineteenth century, but by the time Frith took his photograph it had drifted back again. Today it is kept permanently free, a service often performed in ancient times and by no one more enthusiastically then Pharaoh Tuthmosis IV, who placed a tablet between its paws to record how, in a dream, the Sphinx had told him that the sand was a great nuisance and begged the young prince, as he then was, to remove it.

The Greek Sphinx, a winged lioness, was a sinister deity who became confused with the generally beneficent Egyptian *sheshpankh*, or "living statue," because of the similarity in the sound of their names. The Egyptian Sphinx was a common emblem of royal potency, a lion with the bearded head of a king or of the sun god. It figured prominently in the approaches to temples. The Great Sphinx at Giza was carved by order of Pharaoh Khafra from a knob of rock left in the quarry from

which came the blocks that formed the core of his pyramid. Its worn and blunted features are the result not only of the abrasive action of the sand but of the pockmarks caused by the bullets of the Ottoman rulers' Turkish janizaries, who used it for target practice.

As for the Great Pyramid—what can one say about it? Four hundred and ninety feet high. Two million three hundred thousand blocks of stone, each averaging two and a half tons. A base that covers an area of 31 acres. An interior threaded by a corridor leading to a Queen's Chamber, and a Grand Gallery leading to a King's Chamber, the latter a huge granite room corbeled with seven granite slabs in which reposes a massive royal sarcophagus (alas, empty—looted or never used). Add to all this the fact that the whole exterior was once faced (now only meagerly) with smooth, dazzling slabs of limestone between whose thousandth-of-an-inch joints not even the blade of a knife can be inserted. Truly the sepulchre or cenotaph of a mighty king.

13 ROCK TOMBS AND THE PYRAMID OF KHAFRA

The identity of the individual builders of the pyramids and of other Egyptian monuments was known to Frith, who was acquainted with the work of Emil Brugsch and other scholars. Champollion had deciphered hieroglyphic writing, with the help of the Rosetta Stone, in the 1820s, and had published his grammar and dictionary; and by 1850 the true science of Egyptology had been firmly established by such men as Brugsch, Lepsius, Birch, Chabas, de Rougé, and above all by the legendary Auguste Mariette, pioneer excavator and conservator, first director of the Cairo Museum, raised to the rank of Bey by the Khedive Ismail. This distinguished band would soon be joined by scholars of the caliber of Erman, Sethe, Breasted, Garstang and Petrie. Nevertheless, Frith was still close enough to Egyptology's earliest and heroic age to call Khafra's pyramid by the old-fashioned names of "Second Pyramid," "Middle Pyramid" or "Belzoni's Pyramid" after the remarkable Italian, once a circus strongman, who was the first European to hew his way into it in 1816.

Belzoni was not deterred by the presence in temples and tomb chambers of bats and wild beasts or by stories of ghosts. In the present photograph it is interesting to see the caves in the foreground comfortably occupied by squatters. As a general rule, the average Arab was very wary, as he still is today, about lingering among the lonelier monuments of his ancient Egyptian predecessors, such as the Giza pyramids were then. In particular Arabs avoided them at night, when the more fearsome and bloodthirsty *afreets* or demons roamed abroad. Only nomads, bandits and professional tomb robbers were reckless or desperate enough to approach the eerie precincts of the departed pharaohs. In the case of temples, whose function was not primarily concerned with death and burial, things were different; people would lose their fear of them and, taking safety in numbers, would put them to use as family dwellings or communal apartment houses.

14 THE VALLEY OF THE NILE FROM THE QUARRIES AT TURA

Tura, a village on the east bank of the Nile, 12 miles south of Cairo on the road to Helwan, was the source of the gleaming white limestone that sheathed the monuments of the Third and Fourth Dynasties. No doubt its quarries also supplied the material for the renowned White Walls of the nearby city of Memphis. One of the proudest boasts of Weni, a trusted courtier of Pharaoh Pepi I of the Sixth Dynasty, inscribed in Weni's tomb at Abydos, is that: "I begged his sacred Majesty to bring me a sarcophagus of white limestone from Tura, whereat he ordered the chancellor to set sail with mariners and laborers to fetch it for me. . . . The king had never done anything of the kind before for any other subject."

Frith's commentary at this point is very racy and evocative, and its opening paragraph deserves to be quoted in full:

"We have now done with Cairo—have seen the last of its striped mosques and its fantastically beautiful minarets; its ricketty houses and ruin heaps—the grandeur of the past and the meanness of the present. We have worn out two or three gloriously exciting ever-memorable days on the Field of Pyramids and Tombs. We are not satisfied by any means; were our lives of antediluvian measure, we would surely have devoted one entire year to our cane-bottomed chair on the portico of Shepherd's Hotel. These solemn, fusty, loose-twisted old Arabs, whose bare legs eternally act pendulum to the movement of their nodding pit-a-pating donkeys—that imperturbable Turk, covered with braid and buttons, upon a gilt and jewelled saddle, upon a cloth of crimson and gold, upon a great stately ass, sixteen hands high and worth eighty golden guineas—those *pushing* young tradesmen, the donkey-boys, with Murillo faces, and four or five tongues a-piece—Arabic, English, *American*, French, Italian—with backs as brown and dusty as their beasts, as *whackable*, and almost as insensitive—those shabby, tassely, furtive-looking vagabonds, the Bedouin, with their strings of half-starved, grumbling, disjointed camels—oh! to see such stage effects, and hundreds more—unutterably well done—pass by you in eternal sunshine, one little year out of nine hundred were short allotment indeed!"

15   DENDERA: THE PORTICO OF THE TEMPLE

After sailing upriver from Tura, Frith did not photograph another antiquity for almost 350 miles, until he reached the temple of Dendera on the east bank, where the river makes a crank eastward before sweeping south again to Thebes.

"With the exception of the Portico of Esneh," he writes, "which was exhumed by order of Mahommed Ali, Dendera is the first temple ruins which the traveller sees on his way up to Thebes." He might perhaps have paused, on his way through Middle Egypt, to photograph the great rock tombs of the rulers of the Oryx Nome at Beni Hasan, abutting the river and accessible from it; perhaps also the visible remains of the ancient cities of Herakleopolis Magna and Hermopolis Magna; but it is true that at that date such sites as Cynopolis and Lycopolis, and above all the great desert capital of Akhenaton and Nefertiti at Amarna, were either unexplored or unidentified or were in such a bad state that they scarcely warranted the expenditure of Frith's precious stock of plates.

His one surprising and, from our point of view, regrettable omission is the great temple of Seti I at Abydos. True, the temple is set back a few miles from the river, but it is rather mystifying how, 50 miles before he came to Dendera, Frith could have sailed right past one of Egypt's most important and beloved monuments without apparently noticing it.

Dendera, standing in the desert opposite the town of Qena, was an ancient provincial capital, where the cow goddess Hathor had been worshipped from the earliest times. Her head with its cow's ears can be seen in the capitals of the columns in the picture (the entire temple has since been cleared of the encroaching sand). Her shrine at Dendera, with its endless portraits of her, dates mainly from the very end of the pharaonic period, having been begun in the reign of one of the last pharaohs of all, Ptolemy IX, who reigned between 107 and 88 B.C., little more than half a century before Egypt became a Roman province.

16 DENDERA: SCULPTURED RELIEFS

So powerful was Hathor's cult that she was worshipped for 4000 years, from predynastic times until well beyond the extinction of the native dynasties. She was the origin of the Greek Aphrodite, with shrines in Nubia, Egypt, Palestine and Syria. Tender and compassionate, she was the ruler of the sky, mother of Horus, nurse of Pharaoh, patroness of childbearing, music and dancing.

A temple to Hathor had been erected at Dendera by Khufu, builder of the Great Pyramid. Among later pharaohs, Mentuhotep I, founder of the Eleventh Dynasty (ca. 2133 B.C.), dedicated a small chapel that was excavated and later reerected outside the Cairo Museum. Among the names and representations on the walls of the main, Ptolemaic temple are those of Cleopatra and Caesarion, her son by Julius Caesar, and of the Roman emperors Augustus, Tiberius, Caligula, Claudius, Nero, Domitian and Trajan.

Frith's photograph, depicting a section of the exterior wall, demon-strates the brilliant relief into which the bright steady sun of Egypt threw the carvings and statuary of the ancient monuments, and how artfully the sculptors and painters took full advantage of it.

The gods and goddesses depicted in the middle register are, from left to right, Hathor, Amon-Ra, Osiris, Pharaoh (identified by the car-touches as the Emperor Augustus), Mut (wife of Amon), Horus, Maat (goddess of truth), and Hathor again.

Frith found Dendera "forsaken by the peasantry" because the inde-fatigable Mariette had driven out the Arabs who had taken up residence on its roof, its lower reaches being packed with the dirt and rubbish that had provided them with a floor. Such had been the fate of many of Egypt's finest temples since Coptic times, over a thousand years before. Ironically, this undignified treatment often preserved the temples from worse forms of abuse, or from outright demolition.

17   KARNAK: THE COURT OF SHESHONQ I

Frith has now brought us to Thebes, the city which about the year 2000 B.C., when Upper Egypt succeeded Lower Egypt in the leadership of the Two Lands, supplanted Memphis as the wealthiest and most powerful city in the kingdom.

During protodynastic and early dynastic times, Thebes enjoyed a modest prestige as the capital of one of Egypt's 38 major nomes or provinces. Then, as a result of its nomarchs heading the successful national resistance against the foreign invaders called the Hyksôs, in the Eleventh Dynasty it became the capital of the reconstituted realm. During the ensuing Middle Kingdom its local deity, Amon, became head of the Egyptian pantheon. He was united with the sun god Ra and became the war god under whom the armies of the Middle Kingdom and the New Kingdom swept southward into Nubia, and northward deeper and ever deeper into Asia, until the standard of the King of the Gods was planted on the banks of the Euphrates. To the Greeks and Romans, Thebes was Diospolis Magna, the Great City of Zeus.

On the east bank of the Nile at Thebes stood the temples of Karnak and Luxor; on the west bank were palaces, funerary temples and, from the beginning of the New Kingdom onward, the resting place of Egypt's kings, queens and great nobles. Even the kings of the interloping dynasties, the Nubians, Libyans and Persians, the Greeks and the Romans, came personally to Thebes to confirm their position and to place their personal mark on its mighty monuments.

Such an interloper was Sheshonq I (935–914 B.C.), first of the Libyan chiefs who constituted the Twenty-second and Twenty-third Dynasties, an epoch of unease and even chaos. Sheshonq, the Shishak of the Book of Chronicles, was descended from a line of humble desert nomads, the Meshwesh, who had settled in the Delta and gradually rose to supreme power. To give himself status and respectability, Sheshonq erected the great sandstone pylon or gateway that fronts the temple of Karnak, the largest and most venerable of the Theban temples.

18   KARNAK: THE EXTERIOR OF THE GREAT HALL

Frith had been told by a "photographic friend" whom he had met at Cairo that the Great Hall at Karnak was "impregnable—that it was idle to plant a camera against it—such vast and shapeless masses of ruin packed together as tight as it would stow, and built in on all sides with tremendous blank walls. I say I was discouraged; nevertheless, I brought up my artillery boldly, and fired away right and left . . . ."

The temple of Karnak, even today, when much of it has been cleared and put back into some semblance of order, is a place where the visitor can easily lose his bearings. Its sheer size and complexity mask the fact that it follows essentially the simple concept and ground plan of the standard Egyptian temple. A temple was designed to be the god's house or estate, where he lived with his divine family and his mortal servants around him, surrounded by all the appurtenances of a great lord, complete with herds, fields of grain, workshops, cattle sheds and granaries. The temple was not only an estate, but also a center of learning, education and cultural activity, a self-contained world that was often

of enormous extent. Karnak, the world's largest religious edifice still extant (though the ruined Labyrinth, in the Egyptian Fayûm, was once larger still), possessed at its peak, in conjunction with its nearby dependency of Luxor, 90,000 slaves, half a million head of cattle, 400 orchards, 80 ships and 50 workshops, and commanded the revenues of 65 townships in Egypt and Asia.

Nevertheless, despite its swollen proportions, Karnak still adhered to the traditional architectural formula: monumental gate or pylon; the outer courtyard where the god received his guests; his pillared hall, or room of state; and finaly his private apartments, culminating in the small, dark, secret cell where he dwelt in the form of a sacred image which was ceremonially washed, clothed and fed every morning. The fashion in which this basic conception became amplified and obscured at Karnak may be indicated by the fact that the temple came to possess no less than nine pylons.

19   KARNAK: PILLARS IN THE GREAT HALL

What Frith called a columned or pillared hall a modern archaeologist would refer to by the name of a hypostyle hall, denoting a roof resting upon rows of columns.

The great hypostyle hall at Karnak serves as the dominating feature of the entire temple. Its staggering proportions produced an equally staggering effect on Frith when, as he puts it, he "crept round the outer wall, and took advantage of dilapidations therein effected by some former warrior" to take what even at that date he termed his "shots."

The great hall at Karnak is 338 feet wide and 170 feet deep. It consists of 12 central columns in two lines, creating a hall 79 feet high with three central aisles. Flanking the 12 gargantuan drum columns, 12 feet in diameter, with their campaniform or open-papyrus capitals, are 61 smaller columns with papyrus-bud capitals, arranged in such a way as to create a transverse aisle.

The author of this gigantic conception, or at least the pharaoh who endorsed it, was the great Eighteenth Dynasty monarch Amenophis III (1417–1379 B.C.), who contributed the 12 central columns. The flanking columns were added in the reign of Seti I of the following dynasty (1318–1304 B.C.), and finishing touches were added by Ramses II (1304–1237 B.C.). Both Seti and Ramses caused huge reliefs of their victories in Libya, Palestine and Syria to be carved on the outer walls. Originally, of course, the murals and the pillars were embellished with garish colors, which added immeasurably to their effect on the mind of the native worshipper or the traveler from abroad.

20 KARNAK: THE INTERIOR OF THE GREAT HALL

Frith was justly proud of this very fine photograph of the interior of the hall. It was not easy to obtain. "Wheeling round my tackle, . . . burning with ambition—yet with much fearfulness—I entered that dark vista which you see in the center of my last picture, and turning down one of the side aisles, I pointed my camera at a double line of those dingy old immensities—indestructible—indescribable, and hitherto deemed impossible! Not so!"

The picture, which depicts one of the central aisles with its campan-

iform columns, shows the stone grilles that allowed light to filter mysteriously down; above the smaller columns in the side aisles were stone slits. At the ground level, however, and with the original ceiling in place, the effect was dim and numinous, as it was intended to be.

As Champollion wrote, after visiting Karnak during his travels in Egypt in 1828–1830: "No ancient or modern people have thought of art or architecture on such a sublime scale, so vast, so grandiose, as the ancient Egyptians. They thought in terms of men a hundred feet tall."

21   KARNAK: THE BROKEN OBELISK

In its heyday, the area behind the Great Hall at Karnak sported four magnificent pairs of obelisks.

One pair was raised by the first great conqueror of the New Kingdom, Tuthmosis I (1525–1512 B.C.); two pairs were raised by his daughter, principal wife, and later pharaoh in her own right, the King-Queen Hatshepsut (1503–1482 B.C.); and a fourth pair was raised by her famous nephew-husband, Tuthmosis III (1504–1450 B.C.). Tuthmosis III had no love for his aunt-wife, who kept him firmly under her thumb until he was freed by her death for a career as Egypt's most spectacular soldier. One of his first acts was to have his late consort's obelisks securely walled around so that only the topmost third was visible to the gaze of spectators.

Frith's photograph shows an obelisk of Tuthmosis I in the background. It is 75 feet high and is cut from a single block of Aswan granite. It is remarkable for its purity of line and for the superb quality of its hieroglyphic inscription. In front of it is a fallen and cracked obelisk of Hatshepsut. The inscription on the latter reads, in part:

"I was seated in my palace, and I was thinking about the god who made me. My heart conceived the desire to erect in his honor two golden obelisks whose points would pierce the sky. I caused them to be erected between the two great pylons of my father Tuthmosis. You, who see these monuments after the passage of long years, will speak of what I have done. You will say: 'We do not know why these needles of gold were erected.' Hearken! I lavished on them bushels of gold, as though I had been pouring out sacks of grain. And when you learn these things, do not say that my work was dedicated to vanity. Say, rather: 'She did these things because she loved to do so.'"

22   KARNAK: OBELISK

Obelisks were customarily erected in pairs, one on each side of a pylon gateway. Most of them were hewn from red granite from the quarries at distant Aswan. They took their origin from sacred sun stones that were revered in the predynastic period, and became particularly popular during the New Kingdom. The pyramidion or sloping segment at the top was fitted with a bronze cap covered with gold leaf or electrum, and sometimes the sides were also sheathed in gold.

At one time hundreds of obelisks stood on the banks of the Nile, but over the centuries most of them were shattered or carried off to other lands. Today less than half a dozen remain upright in the country of their origin. Ancient Egyptian obelisks can be seen in the squares and public gardens of Rome, Paris, London, New York and Istanbul—almost anywhere except in Egypt itself.

23 KARNAK: GENERAL VIEW

Unlike the smaller, more compact and homogeneous Luxor, Karnak grew largely by accretion and almost haphazardly at the hands of a score of ambitious and self-promoting kings. This is a general view of the ruins as they appeared in the 1850s. The sloping fragments on the left are the lower courses of shattered pylons.

Today, the temple has been put back into a fair semblance of order, thanks largely to the efforts of successive generations of French archaeologists working under the auspices of the Egyptian Antiquities Service.

Auguste Mariette, its first director, began the work of reconstruction at Karnak, Luxor and other classic sites, and his work was carried on by his equally distinguished successor, Sir Gaston Maspero. Later reconstruction is associated with the names and the devoted labors of such men as Grébaut, Daressy, Legrain, Pillet and Chevrier; and among the Egyptians who have headed the Service in the past 30 years the name of the late Zaccariah Goneim is particularly well known.

24 LUXOR: THE ENTRANCE

Luxor and Karnak were linked together ceremonially. Every year the image of Amon was taken downstream from Karnak to visit itself in its other guise as the god Min, forerunner of the Greek god Pan. The two temples were physically united by a great *dromos* or ritual avenue, consisting of a double row of sphinxes. The *dromos* (a Greek term) was originally the handiwork of the preeminent Eighteenth Dynasty builder Amenophis III (1417–1379 B.C.) and was reconstituted and extended a thousand years later by Nectanebo I of the Thirtieth Dynasty (380–363 B.C.), one of the last of the ambitious native builders. It is interesting, looking at Frith's photograph, to reflect how at that time the great drift of soil covered up the avenue of sphinxes completely, reaching as high as the shoulders of the colossal statues flanking the gateway. The very existence of the avenue was not suspected until many years later, and final clearance was not effected until the 1950s.

The two colossi, now also freed of earth, are of black granite. They represent Ramses II of the Nineteenth Dynasty (1304–1237 B.C.), Egypt's most grandiose and pertinacious royal builder. Originally the entrance was adorned with four additional statues of the king in rose granite, of which only one now remains in place.

To Ramses II also belongs the obelisk at the left, originally one of a pair. The two obelisks were given to France by Mohammed Ali in 1831, but the French took only the one that was in the better state of preservation and set it up in 1836 in the Place de la Concorde.

Above the right-hand corner of the black oblong mud-brick Arab construction on the left can be seen the top of one of the four deep grooves or sockets in which were fastened the flagpoles with streamers with which the pylon was furnished.

25   LUXOR: THE COURTYARD OF AMENOPHIS III

Luxor owes its harmonious and uncluttered character to the fact that, although minor elements were contributed by earlier or later kings, the temple was almost entirely the handiwork of two pharaohs, Amenophis III and Ramses II.

The photograph shows the splendid courtyard of Amenophis III, one of the most elegant inspirations in the Egyptian canon. It consists of double rows of slender columns topped by the closed papyrus.

The picture is of unusual interest, as it shows in a vivid manner the uses and abuses to which the monuments were subject as recently as a century ago. The piles of what looks like earth which are heaped almost to the tops of the columns are not earth but grain, for here was stored the grain that the government took in taxes from neighboring farmers. The trucks in the picture were not part of an archaeological excavation, as one might suppose at first sight, but were grain tubs. In the radiant and virtually rainless climate of Luxor, such heaps of grain could lie about almost indefinitely without spoiling.

The court has now, of course, been cleared of such obstructions, also of the casual constructions which one can see in the foreground. According to Frith, the precincts of Luxor were particularly noted for such mistreatment. "Around many of the stupendous ruins of Old Egypt are now heaped mountains of the *débris* of deserted towns; or else modern Arab hovels of mud . . . . He must indeed be a hardy antiquarian whose enthusiasm will lead him amongst all its [Luxor's] columns, half of whose height is buried in the garbage and filth of former generations, and the remaining half reeking and swarming with that of the present."

The modern visitor is surprised to see, tucked into a corner of the forecourt, the impeccable little mosque, with its minaret, wherein are interred the bones of an Islamic saint, Abu el-Haggag. The mosque sits squarely on a portion of the ancient temple, blandly resisting the process of historical investigation.

26   LUXOR: THE APPROACH TO THE COURTYARD OF AMENOPHIS III

In order to make his courtyard more impressive, Amenophis placed in front of the pylon that gave entrance to it a double column of pillars, 14 in number, 50 feet high, and roofed across the top. The pillars were massive, with open-lotus capitals, and a second pylon was erected to give additional status to the new approach. The heavy, bulbous character of the pillars is a somewhat painful contrast to the delicate appearance of the columns in the courtyard behind, and are reminiscent of the overblown style of Ramses II. Ramses II, in fact, added his own, larger courtyard to Amenophis III's colonnade, completing it with the pylon featured in Plate 24. Frith's picture shows Amenophis' colonnade and his second pylon.

The charm of the present picture lies in the additional evidence it offers of the activities of the Arab squatters who infested the ancient temples. The dark structures in the left foreground and the smaller whitewashed box tucked away at right center are casual mud-brick Arab hutments of the type swept away by the Antiquities Service.

"The great columns represented in my picture," writes Frith, " . . . will at once be familiar to every Nile traveller; many of whom I have no doubt, with myself, upon landing at Luxor, have found their anxiety for news from home overpowering for a while their antiquarian enthusiasm, and have hurried past the superb columns"—Frith did not share the aesthetic reservations expressed in the opening paragraph above—"in hot haste to the temple of Mustapha-Aga, the native English consular agent, for their letters! Mustapha's abode lies in the shadow on the right of the picture, and he sails into his audience-chamber, in long silken gown and turban, makes his salaam, and hands you all his stock of letters—thirty or forty of them—you can take your choice.

". . . The group of figures in the centre of the picture are natives, who were quarrelling energetically at the moment, and quite unconscious of my designs upon them. The picture was taken in about six seconds."

27   THEBES: THE COLOSSI OF MEMNON

Now Frith has left behind the temples of Karnak and Luxor, with the populous ancient and modern townships that grew up around them, and has taken the ferry across the Nile to the western bank. Here, where the sun "died" every evening beyond the rim of the mountains, the Theban monarchs constructed their mortuary temples and "august places of eternity." Regularly, from the New Kingdom onward, they excavated their tombs and the tombs of their families and courtiers in the hidden valleys reaching back into the hills.

Some pharaohs also erected palaces on the west bank. The famous Colossi of Memnon, for example, are all that remains standing of the great palace temple of Amenophis III, constructed for him by his vizier and master builder, Amenhotep son of Hapu. The king esteemed Amenhotep so highly that he accorded him the privilege, unique in Egyptian annals, of erecting his own mortuary temple. Even Zoser's vizier Imhotep (see Plate 9) and Hatshepsut's favorite Senmut were not granted such an extraordinary honor.

The Colossi of Memnon guarded the entrance to Amenophis III's mortuary temple, perhaps his largest personal enterprise and his architect's masterpiece. It was destroyed in a great earthquake in 27 A.D., which also cracked the Colossi themselves. The statues, which are 65 feet tall, the height of a five-story building, both represent Amenophis III. Beside the king's leg on one statue stands the infinitely smaller figure of his Chief Royal Wife, Tiy, and beside his leg on the other the small figure of his mother, Mutemuya. On the side panels of the throne are carved representations of the androgynous gods of the Northern Nile and the Southern Nile, with their multiple, pendulous breasts. At one time the right-hand or northern colossus, thanks to a fissure produced by the earthquake, emitted every morning in the dawn breeze a singularly sweet and melodious whistle; but the Roman emperor Septimius Severus poked about with the statue to find how the sound was produced, with the result that the statue, offended, fell totally silent thereafter.

28   THEBES: THE TEMPLE OF GURNEH

Gurneh was the most easterly of the mortuary temples on the west bank, and the one nearest the river.

It was intended to serve the cult of Seti I, who made good progress with it in his lifetime, but was completed by his son and successor Ramses II, who on the colonnade leading to the inner chambers (shown in the picture) recorded that "he made this as a monument to his father, the dead Seti I, and to his grandfather, the dead Ramses I." Many kings, including Ramses II himself, were not always so pious, blithely chiseling from temples, tombs, statues, obelisks and even sarcophagi the names of their predecessors or rivals and substituting their own.

Seti I and Ramses II, monarchs who reigned in the long high noon of the New Kingdom, possessed the leisure and the enormous wealth to build and to restore extensively on the west bank, as Amenophis III had done on the east. The temple at Gurneh originally possessed two pylons and two courtyards and a complex of inner, private shrines of which the colonnade was the facade. The papyrus columns with their bud capitals possess the typically lifeless, perfunctory Ramses II form, and his cartouches, only too familiar to the archaeologist and the traveler, are monotonously repeated over every available space.

29   THEBES: THE RAMASSEUM

Whether or not the architectural style of Ramses II is to one's taste, it is impossible not to be impressed by the Ramasseum. In its heyday, it probably ranked second in size only to Amenophis III's vanished temple, described in Plate 27, and constituted the hub round which radiated the other monuments and the necropolises on the west bank.

Again, as at Gurneh, Ramses II was subjecting his father to his somewhat bear-like embrace. The Ramasseum grew as an addition at the west side of a modest temple of Seti I, eventually swallowing it up in a vast complex of religious constructions and a rambling city of storehouses and workshops.

Even today, in ruin, it strikes the visitor with its ponderous and uncompromising monumentality. It once possessed two courtyards with enormous pylons, supplied with the inevitable colossal statues of the king, a hypostyle hall (which dominates Frith's picture, and of which the lofty pillars of the nave rise above the rest) and the customary congeries of inner shrines and temples.

On both the first and second pylons Ramses caused to be described and portrayed the military triumphs of the early years of his reign, when he was an active campaigner against the Syrians and the Hittites. In particular, he loved to dwell on the events of the fifth year of his kingship, when he defeated the Hittites at the great battle of Kadesh on the river Orontes. Here, the Egyptian army was demoralized and hurled back, and the day was only saved by the king charging in person at the head of his bodyguard. His feat was commemorated by a poet called Pentawer in a tedious epic, which must have bored generations of Egyptian schoolchildren as much as the enormous self-congratulatory murals of the victory-snatched-from-disaster that the king caused to be scattered through the length and breadth of his dominions. They are not only a chief feature of the Ramasseum but are reiterated on a similar scale on the walls of Karnak, Luxor and Abu Simbel.

30   THEBES: THE FALLEN COLOSSUS AT THE RAMASSEUM

The colossus in Frith's photograph lay, and still lies, in the first courtyard, its debris being scattered along the whole of one side of the court. It was originally carved from a single block of syenite, brought from a quarry 100 miles distant and weighing 900 tons, or three times as much as any of the obelisks at Karnak. It may be the largest single statue ever carved. All that remains standing is its pedestal.

The early and mid-Victorians, with their inheritance from the Romantics, felt a special awe in the contemplation of such fallen grandeur. It may have been a description of this statue or an engraving of it in an account by an early traveler that inspired Shelley to write about Ozymandias and the "vast and trunkless legs of stone." The Greco-Roman historian Diodorus Siculus, writing in the first century B.C., believed that the Ramasseum was the burial place of the legendary Egyptian potentate Ozymandias, and it seems altogether likely that the name was a Greek corruption of the name Wesermaatra-Ramses, prenomen and nomen of Ramses II. So Ramses the Great is, fittingly, Ozymandias.

"Look on my works, ye mighty, and despair!"

Besides the term Ramasseum, the term Memnonium was in use for the edifice in Frith's day. "Memnon" was another Greek corruption, or rather misunderstanding, of a word which Greek travelers had picked up in Egypt. It was an attempt to pronounce the word which the Egyptians applied to any religious object or religious building, but the Greeks thought it applied to some particular king; hence Colossi of Memnon.

Neither Ramses II's 16 years of warfare against the Syrians and Hittites, nor his campaign against the Libyans and Nubians, saved Egypt from the collapse and disintegration that were soon to overtake it: indeed, his megalomania and extravagance can only have helped to bring them on. Nevertheless, the reign of Ramses the Great, as Frith and the Victorians called him, which lasted for 67 years and ended when Ramses was almost 100 years old, can justly be considered the last great flowering of Egyptian genius and prosperity.

31   THEBES: THE TEMPLE-PALACE OF MEDINET HABU

Medinet Habu, a short distance southwest of the Colossi of Memnon, survived the earthquake that destroyed the temple of Amenophis III which those statues once guarded. (Amenophis III experienced other posthumous ill fortune on the west bank of the river, for his immense palace called Malkata, a sprawling rabbit warren of a place that grew haphazardly over the years, is now also thoroughly shattered.)

The temple-palace of Medinet Habu, better preserved than the Ramasseum, is of almost identical plan and dimensions. Dwarfing the earlier royal temples on the same site, it constituted both the mortuary temple and the secular palace of Ramses III (1198–1166 B.C.): his house of death and his house of life. Around them he threw up two walls, one over 30 feet thick and 60 feet high, and two towering gateways of which one, three stories high, has survived.

Ramses III of the Twentieth Dynasty ruled Egypt for 32 years. He was an able and determined man who deserves the title of "the Great" as least as much as his namesake. He turned back a determined Libyan invasion, defended the frontiers of the Empire in Asia and Nubia, and held in check the ceaseless attempts of the Sea Peoples—a ruthless and well-armed congeries of nomads who were turning the Mediterranean world upside down—to effect a foothold in Egypt. In particular his navy inflicted on the flotillas of the Sea Peoples a crushing defeat which he caused to be depicted on the walls of Medinet Habu, together with representations of the huge numbers of foreign prisoners taken captive by his forces. Graphically portrayed by the sculptor, these prisoners provide a fascinating catalogue of the myriad tribes and nationalities of the epoch.

But the threat to the king was not only external. At the very close of his long life he escaped an attempt at assassination at the hands of conspirators headed by his own son and one of his wives: a sad end to a distinguished reign—the last unequivocally great reign in the history of the native dynasties.

32   THEBES: THE PYLON GATEWAY AT MEDINET HABU

The quality of workmanship of Medinet Habu compares favorably with that of the Ramasseum. To the left of the gateway, effectively photographed by Frith, can be seen the figures of some of the foreign captives referred to in the commentary to the previous plate.

The registers on the side panels of the gateway show Ramses III adoring the various gods of Thebes. The king, arms lifted, wears a number of different crowns—White Crown, Red Crown, *atef* crown— as he offers a libation to Osiris (backed in one register by Ra, in another by Isis), to Amon with his high-feathered crown, and to the ithyphallic god Min, whose cult became prominent at Thebes.

One might mention that, on the exterior wall of the second hypostyle hall, is an exceptionally lively frieze of the king in his chariot conducting an exciting hunt of wild bulls.

33 THEBES: THE INTERIOR OF MEDINET HABU

A view of the grand hypostyle hall, with its 24 columns and its side chapels and treasuries, after preliminary clearance.

Some of Frith's observations on this particular plate are exceedingly amusing and picturesque:

"In a previous article upon a portion of this temple . . ., written on my first journey, occurs the following:—'The place is dreadfully encumbered with heaps of shapeless ruin, and still more with perfect mountains of the debris of deserted Arab towns, under which the further portions of the great temple are absolutely buried. One can only guess how much more of magnificence and interest might reward the efforts of a vigorous excavating party.'

"On my late visit, I found that such efforts had been rewarded to the extent which I have now the pleasure to represent. The whole of this fine court, or hall of columns, with a number of lateral ante-chambers, had been excavated by order of the Pasha, whose object in these works was two-fold; first, to stock a fine museum which he has lately erected at Cairo, somewhat after the style of the Crystal Palace, and executed in France; and secondly, to earn the commendations of travellers and of the civilized world. In the first of these objects he has had tolerable success, although, it is to be feared, that a great proportion of the portable valuables discovered find their way into other collections than that at Cairo. I take considerable exception also to the manner in which his works have been executed. In some instances, noble masses of picturesque ruin have been blown to pieces, and removed without any idea of uncovering objects of interest, but simply to clear the space. The material to be removed is, however, chiefly the unburnt brick of Arab ruins, and an incredible accumulation of fine dust. The 'hands' employed are generally children, who are 'pressed' from the adjoining villages. They carry out the dust in baskets upon their heads, and their movements are continually accelerated by 'taskmasters' armed with *corbashes,* or whips of hippopotamus hide, which are capable of inflicting a terrible stroke."

34   THEBES: THE ENTRANCE TO THE VALLEY OF THE KINGS

Dominating the western bank of the river is the natural landmark of the Theban Peak. It bears such a striking resemblance to a pyramid that in the eyes of the ancient Egyptians it rendered the region of the great necropolis truly holy ground.

The most southerly of the burial places was the Valley of the Queens, flanked by the private cemeteries in which lay the tombs of the great nobles, the temple and tombs of Deir el-Medina, and—in the region of the temple of Gurneh—the cemeteries of Abu el-Neggah. In the plain before Queen Hatshepsut's temple of Deir el-Bahari were the cemeteries of Sheik Abd el-Gurnah and Assassif; but it was immediately behind Deir el-Bahari that in a sheltered and transverse fold or *wadi* in the hills lay the Eastern Valley or Valley of the Kings, which housed the bones of no less than 61 of the rulers of Egypt, from Tuthmosis I to Ramses IX. Another four kings, including Amenophis III, were interred in the even more inaccessible Western Valley beyond. Of all these tombs, only that of Tutankhamon was found intact, and together with Amenophis II he is one of the only two kings whose remains still lie in the Biban el-Muluk or Gates of the Kings, as the Arabs call the Eastern Valley.

Only 27 of the tombs in the Eastern Valley had been located when Frith took his photograph of the entrance of "the deep and romantic gorge" where there was no "sign of life except when a solitary vulture wheels overhead, or a jackal is seen stealing away amongst the hot loose stones." A change from today, with the asphalted roads, the busloads of tourists, and the files of guides and policemen. Frith visited some of the tombs, and was particularly struck, as visitors are today, by the huge hypogeum of Seti I, with its descending staircases, multiple rooms and lavish murals. We can visualize his frustration at his inability to capture its fascinating interior with the equipment of the time.

35 ERMENT: CLEOPATRA'S "BIRTH TEMPLE"

Frith's well-composed photograph is nonetheless a sad one; four years after he took it, these particular temple ruins were dismantled by order of the Khedive Said, whose thirst for modernizing brought about the building of the first railways and the commencement of the Suez Canal. The temples of Erment, like many temples elsewhere, were toppled and their blocks and pillars ground down to provide building materials for a local sugar factory.

Erment or Armant, ancient Hermonthis, was already an important site in protohistoric and predynastic times, and preceded Thebes, a few miles to the north, as capital of the Sceptre Nome. Here Mentuhotep I built a temple to the war god Montu, to which extensive additions were made by the kings of the New Kingdom, and building went on until the end of the Late Period. Nectanebo II (360–343 B.C.) erected

a temple, and Cleopatra (51–30 B.C.) the *mammisi* or "birth temple" of Montu shown in the photograph. A *mammisi,* a term invented by Champollion, was an annex in Late Period temples wherein was annually celebrated the birth of the god. Other examples exist at Dendera (Hathor), Edfu (Horus) and Philae (Isis). In the nearby necropolis existed an extraordinary subterranean labyrinth or Bucheum in which the white bulls sacred to Montu were buried in enormous sarcophagi. These bull burials continued into the reign of Diocletian (284–305).

Cleopatra's cartouche can be seen on the block at the upper left. The words "Cleopatra" and Ptolemy" were the two first words to be deciphered by Champollion in 1822, and it is melancholy to have lost, at Erment, another trace of the existence of that remarkable and courageous woman.

36 THE TEMPLE OF EDFU

At Edfu, 60 miles south of Luxor, stands the magnificent temple of Edfu, the best preserved of all the monuments of ancient Egypt. Here Horus, the child of Isis and Osiris, was worshipped in several forms—as a falcon, as a human being with a hawk's head, as a winged disk—and under several names: Horus, Horus-Ra, Horus the Brave, Horus the Golden, Horus the Behdetite. His exploits, particularly his mighty battle against his uncle Set, are enshrined on its walls. Every year his wife Hathor (see Plates 15 & 16) made a solemn journey up the Nile to pay him a visit.

Edfu, like many towns with Late Period temples, had been prominent from early times, as the capital of the Seat of Horus Nome, but the great temple as it now exists was exclusively a Ptolemaic creation. We know the exact date of its inception, August 23, 237 B.C., in the reign of Ptolemy III Euergetes, and the date of its completion, in 57 B.C., in the reign of Ptolemy IX Auletes. We know also the name of the architect who designed it: Imhotep, a namesake of the architect of Zoser. Its design is simple and traditional, but because of the general disturbances that went on in the epoch of the Greek rulers it took 180 years to bring it to a faithful and triumphant conclusion.

The temple consists of the 118-foot-high pylon shown in Frith's picture, a fine colonnaded courtyard, two hypostyle halls, two inner chambers with ten side chapels, and a sanctuary or Holy of Holies. The complex is exactly 450 feet long and 259 feet wide and is surrounded by a massive enclosure wall. The temple stairways are all in a satisfactory condition, and it is delightful to climb them to obtain views of the temple and the surrounding sweep of countryside. The French troops of Napoleon's ill-fated campaign of 1799 found its aerial panorama attractive, and so many of them carved their names on top of the pylon that one of them boasted: "All the names inscribed on this monument are French." (These were the same troops who, on their way upriver, are said to have been so overwhelmed by their first sight of the temple of Karnak that they halted as one man and presented arms.)

37   GEBEL SILSILEH

Frith, in his voyage southward from Erment to Edfu, had paused at Esna, but did not photograph the temple there. He found that it was almost "entirely buried in the débris of modern houses," except for the portico which had been cleared a decade earlier. This is a pity, as subsequent excavation has revealed the existence of a splendid and well-preserved hypostyle hall with 24 graceful columns that the Emperors Claudian and Vespasian had added to the Ptolemaic portico. Titus, Domitian, Nerva, Hadrian, Antoninus Pius, Septimius Severus and Caracalla all depicted themselves on its walls in the dress of Egyptian pharaohs, and the latest of its highly original series of texts dates from the reign of Decius (about 250 A.D.).

Nor did Frith stop at El-Kab, ten miles north of Edfu, to record any of the great sprawl of buildings, with their huge rampart, raised during a period of 3000 years, from the Old Kingdom to Ptolemaic times.

On the other hand, he records his pleasure in later stopping his boat among the mountains of the Gebel Silsileh, where in ancient times a chain could be stretched across two rocks in a narrow stretch of the river to halt invaders or to demand toll.

Silsileh was ancient Egypt's chief source of sandstone, and among its quarries were scattered innumerable small chapels and stelae carved out by the men of the expeditions who labored there. Frith depicts in his plate the little rock-hewn chapel cut out of the sandstone during the reign of Tutankhamon's formidable military successor Horemhab (1348–1320 B.C.). Inside is a lively scene depicting Horemhab conducting one of his triumphant campaigns.

38   THE TEMPLE OF KOM OMBO

Kom Ombo, ancient capital of the To-Seti Nome, possessed the usual cluster of earlier temples which either degenerated of their own accord, during the long progress of Egyptian history, or were demolished in order to make way for a more imposing temple in the Ptolemaic era.

Frith's photograph shows the lovely setting of Kom Ombo, unsurpassed among the surviving monument sites of ancient Egypt. One's boat anchors at the foot of the temple itself, which is approached by a flight of steps and a short path. The grand sweep of the Nile, above which the temple stands, can be seen at the right of the picture.

Kom Ombo resembles Dendera, Edfu and other Ptolemaic temples in Upper Egypt in its overall plan, though it has not survived in comparably intact condition. In the main it was the work of Ptolemy VI Philometor, Ptolemy VIII Euergetes II, Ptolemy XI Neos Dionysos, and Cleopatra's son Caesarion; while Augustus, Tiberius and Claudius contributed reliefs and there is a representation of Domitian on the outer wall.

The most interesting feature of the temple is its double or binary character. A number of gods and goddesses were allotted small chapels, but one half of the temple was dedicated principally to the cult of the falcon-headed god Horus the Great, whom the Greeks called Haroeris, and the other half to the crocodile god Sebek or Sobk. Elaborate rituals were evidently celebrated in connection with these two deities and their divine families. This resulted in the curious architectural doubling of all the gates, entrances and shrines.

39 KOM OMBO: A CLOSER VIEW

The sorry state of Kom Ombo when Frith visited it is evident in the photograph. Dirt and sand reached almost to the tops of the columns, while the huge blocks balanced on top of them were sliding and teetering. It is pleasant to report that today the rubbish has been cleared away and the fine sharp lines of the building can be discerned and admired.

A great variety of columns and capitals were employed in Ptolemaic temples, some of which are shown in the picture. On the right is a slender column with a feathery palm capital, while the others terminate in fanciful composite capitals.

"Immediately behind the temple," Frith writes, "I shot my first Egyptian hare, rather small, but well-flavoured. I also saw several coveys of very wild partridges. Stretching away to the south are extensive plantations of the castor-oil plant, cotton fields, &c."

40   Crocodile on a Sandbank

This is one of the very few studies by Frith that portray any form of wild life—though of course such studies were almost out of the question with the facilities available to him. Crocodiles, however, were patient sitters, and one is reminded of the remark by Oscar Wilde, a photographic enthusiast, that "Cows are very fond of being photographed, and, unlike architecture, don't move."

Frith's crocodile certainly looks pleased enough at having his picture taken; but one gives Frith high marks for courage, all the same, for coming so close to the beast in those days before the telephoto lens had been thought of. He wrote: "I am satisfied that they never attack mankind openly, although, no doubt, if they had an opportunity of seizing a man without exposing themselves, they would be dangerous." He did not go so far as the eccentric nineteenth-century English naturalist Squire Wharton, who actually took a ride, complete with reins and saddle, on a crocodile's back.

The ancient Egyptians, like the Egyptians of Frith's time, certainly believed the crocodile was lethal, and sought to placate it. Under the guise of the crocodile god Sebek or Sobk, the Greek Suchos, it was considered a partner of the malign god Set, who had murdered his brother Osiris, and it was worshipped principally at Kom Ombo and at Crocodilopolis in the Fayûm. At Crocodilopolis the sacred crocodiles were given special food, their ears were adorned with golden pendants, bracelets were fastened around their front feet, and when they died they were embalmed and placed in elaborate coffins. "The Aggressor," as he was called, was also honored with many now-lost temples in the Delta, among whose swamps he was plentiful. By Frith's time, however, the wise beast had already retreated upriver as far as Middle Egypt, though Frith states that he shot an adventurous specimen not far south of Cairo. Today there are no crocodiles on the Egyptian stretch of the Nile, and they have retired to the Sudan, well below the temple of Abu Simbel.

41 ASWAN

Aswan, the Greek Syene, less than 50 miles north of the Tropic of Cancer, is situated where the smooth flow of the river breaks up to bubble over the fast rapids that constitute the First Cataract. It was the capital of ancient Egypt's first nome or administrative district. From its quarries came the granite for the monuments and for the lands around it for more than 3000 years. Aswan was also the entrepôt for the ships and caravans of the pharaohs and merchant princes trading with Nubia, the Red Sea and the interior of Africa; on its stone wharves were unloaded slaves, ivory, ebony, exotic animals and birds, ostrich feathers, spices, furs, scarce woods and other rare commodities.

The ancient township stood at the point where Frith took his picture and on the nearby island of Elephantine, once connected to the shore by a bridge. There, and on the other islands of Seheil and Bige, the pharaohs of the Old, Middle and New Kingdoms raised important temples, and everywhere were tablets and memorials to commemorate the kings and other travelers who made the long voyage to Syene and Elephantine. For Aswan was an unusually holy site. Hathor was wor-shipped here as the Mistress of Nubia. Here dwelt Khnum, the ram-headed god who fashioned the world on his potter's wheel. In a secret cave the god of the Nile, Haapi, regulated the flow of the waters and the height of the annual flood. Above all, Osiris himself, watched over by the faithful Isis, slept his last sleep in his tomb called the Abaton, on the little island of Bige.

The ancient Egyptian, no less than the modern visitor, would fail to recognize bustling and prosperous Aswan in the poor and humdrum scene portrayed by Frith. The modern tourist would recognize only the enduring shape of the Nile boats or *feluccas,* with their slanting fore-masts. Aswan was to be discovered as a wintering place in late Victorian times, when the elegant Old Cataract Hotel was constructed. In recent years it has been joined by the New Cataract Hotel, by the Nile Hilton and by others, as Aswan continues to grow into an important resort and an industrial town behind the bulwark of the Sadd el-Aali, the High Dam, with its potential billion kilowatts of power and its 2000-square-mile lake.

42　Philae: the Approach

Noting that "everybody has sketched it—many clever artists have painted it—Murray has engraved it for his 'Guide,' " Frith was still confident that the beauty of this famous scene was such that it would not be devalued by what he called the "unflattering mechanical picture-making" of his camera.

Here the temple of Philae rose "like a vision of a giant fairy-land, from the midst of these weird stones and waters." The temple, he said, "is the most beautiful thing in Egypt": and the majority of Victorian travelers would have agreed with him.

Philae, one of the cluster of islands at Aswan, where the Nile narrows and rattles over the cataract, was not built upon until the reign of Nectanebo I (380–363 B.C.) of the Thirtieth Dynasty, Egypt's last native dynasty. It was then left to the Ptolemies of the Greek dynasty to build the temple of Isis, which in turn became surrounded—one might almost say festooned—with a cluster of exquisite buildings for which the emperors of Rome made themselves responsible. Tiberius, Claudius, Trajan, Marcus Aurelius, Lucius Verus and Diocletian all caused loving additions to be made in and around the temple itself. The quality of Roman Imperial work in Egypt, as exemplified at Philae, is an indication of the care and resources they were willing to lavish on their Egyptian dependency, and the seriousness with which they took their role as the heirs of the pharaohs.

Philae, in fact, acquired a reputation as the last stubborn refuge of the worship of the old gods. The temples of Philae were not officially banned from carrying out their venerable rituals until the reign of the Emperor Justinian (527–565 A.D.), and pilgrims were still carving hymns and prayers to Isis on the walls as late as 473 A.D.

43 PHILAE: PHARAOH'S BED

Pharaoh's Bed was the quaint name for this, the most attractive of the pendant jewels of the temple of Isis, standing a little apart from it on the west of the island.

It is in fact the Kiosk of the Emperor Trajan (about 100–117 A.D.). It adorned one of the landing places of the island, and may have been intended as a resting place for bodies arriving at or leaving Philae. It was originally roofed with a painted ceiling of cedarwood, and according to some ancient writers its campaniform columns were additionally adorned with Hathor heads. Inside are reliefs depicting Isis, Osiris and Horus, with Trajan in the garb of a pharaoh making offerings to them.

44 PHILAE: THE SOUTH END OF THE ISLAND

As a modern photographer would put it, this is a reverse-angle shot of Plate 42.

One of the most ambitious projects put in hand during the years of the British protectorate (1882–1922) was the construction of the Nile barrage at Aswan. It began in 1899, was inaugurated in 1902, and was twice expanded in the years 1907–1912 and 1932–1934. As a result, the temple of Philae was completely submerged beneath the waters for the greater part of the year, and only rose slowly into total visibility during the hot months of July and August, when the reservoir of the barrage reached its lowest point. Strangely, this odd and romantic process does not appear to have harmed the temple.

The island of Philae is now covered permanently by the waters of Lake Nasser, but a large-scale rescue operation mounted in 1960 removed most of the monuments to higher ground before the island was submerged.

45   PHILAE: SCULPTURES IN THE TEMPLE

Frith was so impressed by Philae that, like most Victorian painters and photographers, he made more studies of it than of any other Egyptian monument.

This fine plate shows the sculptures on the outer gateway, with some typical Nubians posed to give the scale. The carved figures are those of Isis and her son Horus. Isis reached Philae after exhaustive travels throughout Egypt, Nubia and the eastern Mediterranean, recovering the remnants of her husband Osiris' body after they had been dismembered and scattered to the four winds by his assassin, Set. Her task completed, she deposited the remains in the Abaton (see text to Plate 41), watching over them and resting there after her labors. Horus can be seen wearing the *pschent:* the flat red crown of Lower Egypt combined with the tall white conical crown of Upper Egypt. Beneath this Double Crown can be seen the twisted horns of the ram god Khnum, since Khnum was the resident god of Elephantine (and indeed vast flocks of goats swarming over the rocks were a common spectacle in ancient times). Besides

being a creator god, Khnum was also one of the guardians who watched over the sources of the Nile.

The damage that can be seen on Isis' face was caused by one of the roaming bands of Christian fanatics during the Coptic epoch (323–641 A.D.). Christianity became the state religion of Egypt and the rest of the Empire under Constantine, surviving in Egypt until the Arab conquest. During the three Coptic centuries, Christian sects proliferated throughout the Nile valley and its environs, founding monasteries and great seats of learning. Unfortunately their more extreme adherents made forays into the ancient temples with hammers, chisels and crowbars, seeking to efface as much as possible of the old religion. They inflicted appalling damage, and one can only console oneself with the thought that they did not possess dynamite.

The slot in which one of the flagpoles was inserted and was held in place with metal bands can be clearly seen between the two figures.

46   THE TEMPLE OF KERTASSI

Frith not only journeyed through Lower Nubia, the 300-mile stretch of the Nile that lies between the First Cataract at Aswan and the Second Cataract at Wadi Halfa, just inside the border of modern Sudan: he penetrated beyond the Second Cataract into Upper Nubia and got to within 30 miles of the Third Cataract in what was then called Ethiopia, but is now in the northern province of that enormous country Sudan, more than twice the size of Egypt itself.

He photographed no less than nine of the temples of Lower Nubia, between Aswan and Abu Simbel. Pictures of four of these temples are reproduced here, in the order in which he would have encountered them. The Nubian temples were the handiwork of the great Theban pharaohs of the New Kingdom, faithfully following the pattern of their Egyptian originals. A number of them were as large and lavish as the examples to the north, but to show all those photographed by Frith would only be to duplicate the style of many of the monuments shown in earlier plates. In point of fact, Egyptian armies had already marched beyond the Second Cataract in the First Dynasty, and the pharaohs of the Middle Kingdom had settled and exploited Nubia as far as the Third

Cataract. In extending and consolidating their sway to the Fourth Cataract, the pharaohs of the New Kingdom were seeking to place the imperial stamp on the vast area of established conquest by the creation of impressive monuments.

In our own time, astounding as it seems, the whole region of what was once called Lower Nubia has ceased to exist. The entire stretch between Aswan and Wadi Halfa has become the 300-mile-long Lake Nasser, whose waters are banking up behind the High Dam. The population of Lower Nubia has been transferred en masse to villages around Kom Ombo. As for the ancient monuments, they have, as a result of enlightened and unprecedented effort, been safely removed elsewhere. For example, the temple of Kertassi, shown in this plate, was brought bodily 30 miles downstream and reerected at Chellal, a few miles from Aswan and accessible from it by a short bus or taxi ride.

The little kiosk in the photograph, now at Chellal, is of the same type and period as Trajan's kiosk at Philae (Plate 43). The important quarries nearby were much worked in Greco-Roman times.

47   GREEK TABLETS AT KERTASSI

These tablets too have been removed to what one might term the open-air museum at Chellal (see previous plate). There are over 50 of them, and they were inserted in the exterior wall of a small grotto. The worn sandstone figure in the niche, representing Isis, was the recipient of the prayers and petitions engraved on the tablets.

The plaques date from the time of the Roman emperors Antoninus, Marcus Aurelius and Severus, when the quarries were in full swing and supplying materials for such late temples as Philae. Despite the Roman occupation, the language of the Egyptian upper classes was still Greek, as under the preceding Ptolemies.

Frith's photograph clearly shows a bold *graffito* on the inner wall of the grotto inscribed by an adventurous Italian in 1818.

48 KALABSHA

The reerection of the temple of Kalabsha, brought more than 40 miles downstream and placed on the same site at Chellal as Kertassi, was a major undertaking. It was the largest of the Lower Nubian temples except Abu Simbel, with pylon, pillared courtyard, hypostyle hall and inner shrines and treasuries. It is of lofty and imposing dimensions, as the picture (taken from the hill behind, with the pylon on the left) clearly shows. It was built during the reign of the Emperor Augustus (30–14 B.C.) on the site of a previous temple of Amenhotep II (1450–1425 B.C.), one of Egypt's most determined conquerors.

49   COLOSSI AND SPHINX AT WADI ES-SEBUA

Seventy miles beyond Kalabsha, and a number of temples later, several of which he photographed, Frith came to Wadi es-Sebua, the Valley of the Lions, so called because from the river to the temple stretched an avenue of sphinxes of which three are shown in the present photograph. He conveys their forlorn and dilapidated air.

The colossi are representations of Ramses II, who dedicated the temple to Amon-Ra and Ra-Harmakis and decorated it with reliefs depicting his victories over the local tribes.

Time and bands of roving Christians in the Coptic era (see Plate 45) have wrought great havoc to the monument, and this and the fact that

it is situated well over 100 miles from Aswan led the authorities who supervised the preservation of the Nubian monuments to remove it, when Lake Nasser was created, only a short distance from its original site to the higher ground above. This has also been done in the case of half a dozen other of the remoter temples, which eventually will adorn the fringes of the enormous lake. Other, smaller temples were actually given as gifts to countries which had assisted in the splendid salvage operation. It was in this way that the Metropolitan Museum in New York acquired the pretty miniature temple of Dendur.

50   THE FACADE OF THE SMALL TEMPLE AT ABU SIMBEL

Every reader will be familiar with the modern epic of the cutting of Abu Simbel into numbered blocks and lifting them to a point 197 feet above the level of the new lake, which otherwise would have drowned it. A coffer dam was built to hold back the water while work proceeded feverishly; the project took four and a half years, cost $36 million (of which the United States contributed $15 million) and was completed almost two years ahead of schedule in 1968. The scope and intensity of the work, carried out as it was with sophisticated modern equipment, only underscores the extraordinary ambitions and abilities of the ancient Egyptian architects and engineers.

Before Abu Simbel received its giant face-lift, one voyaged upstream from the First Cataract. To round the final bend of the river and see the twin temples hanging in the air above one was an unforgettable experience. Today one flies in, boards a bus from the airfield, and is shuttled in and out of the site in a couple of hours. Much is lost.

Both the temples were the work of Ramses II (1304–1237 B.C.; for details of his reign and character, see notes on Plates 29 and 30). They were carved out of the rock, and were both completed before the twenty-fourth year of his reign.

The small temple is situated 200 yards to the north of its mighty companion. Dedicated to Hathor, it was Ramses II's tribute to his favorite wife, Nefertari. Four of the six colossi in the picture represent the king himself, and the other two, by a signal dispensation, show Queen Nefertari in the guise of the goddess Hathor. Hathor is the dominant motif expressed in the temple itself, cut back 90 feet into the cliff. The likeness of Hathor, Mistress of Nubia, also adorns the six square pillars in the interior hallway, and is present in the sanctuary and in the tableaux on the walls.

51 THE FACADE OF THE GREAT TEMPLE AT ABU SIMBEL

Frith shows three of the four giant colossi, 65 feet high, seated at the entrance of the great *speos* (a Greek term), or rock-cut tomb. The king wears the *pschent* or Double Crown (see Plate 45). He smiles; his hands—his forefinger alone is three feet long—lie flat upon his thighs; he is such an image of serene majesty that the shattering of one of the inner colossi from the waist up hardly detracts from the awesome effect.

Above the colossi, not shown in the picture, are the figures of 22 baboons, charmingly rendered. The baboon not only amused the Egyptians because of its human characteristics, but also seemed to them to be both wise and beloved by the gods as it was the first creature to raise its voice in greeting each morning to the sun, to Ra; and Abu Simbel was so situated as to look at its most impressive when it was struck by the first rays of the dawn. On each side of the four statues, standing dutifully beside the throne, are the figures of the monarch's much-loved family: his wife Nefertari (a dignified and lovely representation), his mother Tuyi, his sons and his daughters—a softening domestic touch

in a group of such superhuman dimensions.

Beyond the entrance are a pillared hall, a pillared vestibule, an antechamber and an inner sanctuary driven back to a depth of 200 feet into the hillside. These halls and rooms are flanked by deep side chambers. All of them were hewn from the rock with copper chisels, their edges annealed and hardened with grit. The hall is 57 feet high and 52 feet wide, and on each side are four statues of the king in the guise of Osiris.

Until the early nineteenth century the temples had been entirely covered up for many centuries with the sand which still, as Frith's picture shows, covered half the figures in the 1850s. Burckhardt stumbled on the site by accident in 1813, and as a result of his report Belzoni and three Englishmen spent 15 days in July 1817, at a temperature of between 112 and 116 degrees, personally shifting 50 feet of sand from the doorway in order to effect an entrance.

52   ABU SIMBEL: THE ENTRANCE

The entrance is the black wedge at the bottom of the picture.

In the morning, Ra took the form of a child; in the evening, that of an old man. Here he stands proudly in his niche in his mature manhood as the rays of the sun beat down from the meridian.

In the commentary or "article" to an adjoining plate, Frith gives an amusing account of what a visit to Abu Simbel entailed for the mid-Victorian traveler:

"The temple is sculptured in the face of a sandstone rock, which runs sheer down to the river; and here the traveller who arrives 'in season' usually finds a long line of 'dahibiehs' [Nile houseboats], showing an abundance of gaudy flags and pennants, and occasionally saluting with the customary 'complement' of gunpowder the arrival or departure of a comrade.

"The new arrival, with the help of his opera-glass, observes Brown, Jones, and Robinson, with a party of ladies (they have all been married since their continental tour [a reference to Richard Doyle's picture stories]), toiling through the deep sand to the entrance of the temple; also Lord Henry ——, and two other gentlemen, whom he remembers to have seen on the shady side of Pall Mall, looking much cooler than they do at present; and, as he watches their movements, a great horror seizes him (in spite of his antiquarian enthusiasm) at the idea of exchanging his luxurious cushions for the heavy climb up the steep evasive sand-slope, with the thermometer at 130°. However, the effort must be made; he goes ashore, and arriving at the temple, reduces himself to a sedentary position, and—emboldened by the example of the ladies—executes a *glissade* through the narrow entrance, . . . into the great hall of the temple, where the scanty glimmering of day-light, added to that of his candle, reveals to him the eight colossal Osiridae figures, with arms folded upon their breasts, and the beautiful sculptures which adorn the walls."

53 ABU SIMBEL: COLOSSAL FIGURE

An admirable study of the left outer colossus, the one which in Frith's time was the least obscured by sand.

At the bottom left of the picture can be seen the head of one of the subsidiary statues. It represents one of the children of Ramses II, the princess Nebtawi. According to legend, though there is no reason at all why it should not be the literal truth, the pharaoh possessed 162 known, acknowledged and legitimized offspring. Everything that that king did, after all, he did on the grand scale.

54 THE TEMPLE OF SOLEB

Soleb or Sulb was Frith's southernmost objective. The 130-mile journey upriver from Wadi Halfa had taken him six days. He was now 350 miles from Aswan and 800 miles from Cairo. He was told that no European traveler had visited Soleb for some five years.

Soleb was an impressive monument, though it was in poor condition because it had been constructed of a very friable sandstone. It was 600 feet long and 200 feet wide and possessed two pylons, two colonnaded courts and a hypostyle hall with 28 columns, the remains of which are shown in his photograph. It is the handiwork of Amenophis III, and contains murals depicting that king, the Augustus Caesar of Egypt, with his wife Tiy and his daughters celebrating his 30-year jubilee festival. It is interesting to note that at this temple, as at others, his son Amenophis IV (1372–1354 B.C.), better known to history as Akhenaton, the Heretic King, caused his father's names and titles to be chiseled out wherever they appeared and ordered his own to be substituted.

Likewise he excised the name of Amon and replaced it with the name of the Aton, his own personal version or vision of the appearance of the Sun God.

In the Eighteenth Dynasty, when Egyptian control of Nubia extended as far as Napata on the Fourth Cataract, the office was instituted of Viceroy of Nubia or "Royal Son of Kush." The Nubian viceroys, modeling themselves and their state machinery on that of their royal master, became sub-pharaohs in their own right. They also kept a watch over the growth of the independent Nubian kingdom that began to take shape immediately to the south. In the course of time these Nubian dynasts became increasingly wealthy and powerful in their turn, and in the eighth century B.C., when the Egyptians lost control of their own destinies, reluctantly advanced northward to protect the sacred shrines of Egypt, the homes of the gods whom they themselves worshiped by this time.

55 WADI FERAN

Frith's hardihood and pertinacity are to be admired. We have seen the determination with which he struck as far south as Soleb. We now see him setting out for Palestine across the harsh and inhospitable Sinai, 20,000 square miles of territory that even today possesses a population of less than half a million souls, most of them clustered around the northern coast. But it was not this relatively easy northern route that Frith chose, across the north of the peninsula, through modern El Arish; nor did he take the route across its center, through the Giddi or Mitla passes. Instead, he set out along the longest and southernmost route, so that he could follow in the footsteps of Moses, photograph the peaks of the southern ranges, and visit the great monastery of St. Catherine.

He went by horse, with camels to carry his small tents, his provisions and his photographic gear. It was an arduous journey.

By the time he reached the little Wadi Feran he had already traversed 150 hot, stony miles, with a pause at the little caravan town of Abu Zenima. Feran is a little oasis with palm trees and tamarisks, at the foot of Mount Tahouneh, where the inhabitants from time immemorial have cultivated dates, barley and grain. In its vicinity the expeditions of the ancient pharaohs mined turquoise, and according to tradition the Wadi Feran was the place where Moses prayed on the eve of his successful battle against the Amalekites.

56   INSCRIPTIONS AT THE WADI MOKKATAB

Frith photographed these inscriptions in what he called the "Sinaitic" script in the Wadi Mokkatab, or the "Valley of Writing."

Actually, the inscriptions are written in an Aramaic dialect. They date for the most part from the fourth century A.D. They were probably executed by the members of a religious cell or sanctuary that was an offshoot of the monastery at Feran, in the Wadi Feran (previous plate). The latter was an episcopal seat in the fourth century, but was destroyed at the onset of the Arab conquest.

57 GEBEL MOUSA

Gebel Mousa (or Musa) is 60 miles from the southern tip of the peninsula, equidistant between the Gulf of Suez and the Gulf of Akaba. With the guidance of a monk from the nearby Monastery of St. Catherine, it can easily be climbed in three hours—provided one starts out early enough to avoid the midday heat.

"Mount Sinai" is a collective name for the several peaks of the range.

Gebel Mousa, or "Mount Moses," is 7500 feet high and is said to be (though Gebel Sirbal was the original candidate for that honor) the Mount Sinai on whose summit Moses received the Tablets of the Law.

From its peak one can look eastward and see the Gulf of Akaba shining in the distance: for Moses and his weary Israelites, their first glimpse of the Promised Land.

58   MOUNT HOREB

Or was this other grand peak of the holy mountains the fabled Mount Sinai? . . .

The Arab name of Mount Horeb is Gebel Safsafa. Like Gebel Mousa and other peaks in the same range, such as Gebel Megafa and Gebel Moneiga, it can be climbed with assistance from the nearby monastery.

59 THE MONASTERY OF ST. CATHERINE

Situated under the lee of Gebel Mousa, the Monastery of St. Catherine, small as it is, houses a collection of religious manuscripts, in Syriac, Armenian, Coptic, Georgian and Slavic, that is considered to be the second greatest in the world, ranking only after that of the Vatican. Its 3000 volumes have now been systematically microfilmed.

The monastery has a picturesque history. It was founded by the Emperor Justinian (527–565 A.D.) and his empress Theodora in order to house a casket containing the bones of St. Catherine of Alexandria, and was built on what was thought to be the exact spot where Moses saw the Burning Bush. This, in the Middle Ages, made it a place of special pilgrimage. It has withstood for 14 centuries the shocks of the various armies that have marched, ridden or driven in tanks backward and forward across the Sinai—Arab, Frankish, Turkish, British, Israeli. Its granite walls, in places almost 300 feet high, have repelled many raids and sieges. In Frith's time the visitor, as at Mount Athos in Greece, was still hauled up over the battlements by rope and pulley in one of the baskets that were lowered with provisions for the wandering Bedouin and the needy traveler. The monastery fortifications were kept in good repair. In 1801 General Kléber, Napoleon's surrogate in Egypt and an energetic organizer, lent his troops for a major round of restoration, the results of which can clearly be seen in Frith's picture. When Frith visited the monastery it was under the protection of the Czar of Russia, head of the Orthodox Church and keeper of its sacred places, although Sinai itself was under Turkish suzerainty.

St. Catherine's Monastery is a charming and bewildering congeries of buildings and alleyways interspersed with tiny courtyards. It even includes, as a tribute to the official state religion, a miniature mosque. It possesses its own garden and orchard, and its glory is its Byzantine church into which are crammed Arab mosaics, magnificent Greek and Russian ikons, Western oil paintings, marbles, enamels, chalices, reliquaries and even German candelabras.

60 JERUSALEM: FROM THE MOUNT OF OLIVES

"There are no *roads* in Palestine, but merely mule-tracks between important places—the 'beaten tracks' in which travellers have been content to follow each other from year to year, in order to 'do' Palestine."

One must bear in mind, again, the condition of Palestine in Frith's day and the kind of exertions he had to make to compile his photographic record.

"The only view of Jerusalem which does not disappoint the traveller," he says, "is obtained from the hills on the east or north-east of the city. The view from Mount Scopas [Scopus] is very effective . . . ." This is a panoramic study of the city, which in his time, he writes, was "politically unimportant"; in fact, at that date, the Turks had not even dignified Jerusalem with the status of a provincial capital, or even made

it a municipality. Frith estimated that its total population was "probably above twelve or fourteen thousand, of whom only about five thousand are Mohammedans" (1976 population: 300,000).

For this photograph he set up his camera just below the Church of the Ascension. The picture includes about half of the eastern side of the fine old city wall, about two and a half miles in circumference, completed by Sultan Suleiman I in 1542. In the foreground is the Brook Kidron, running through the Vale of Jehoshaphat. The large mosque at right center is the mosque of Omar, with the towers of the Church of the Holy Sepulchre beyond. The smaller mosque at left center is the el-Aqsa mosque.

Under the wall at the extreme right of the picture is the traditional location of Gethsemane.

61   JERUSALEM: FROM THE CITY WALL

"The present wall of Jerusalem has a parapet walk," writes Frith, "extending nearly all round, and not in any way forbidden to the traveller, excepting in the part which flanks the temple area on the eastern side. This walk is reached from the interior by means of flights of steps placed at convenient distances. One of these flights is seen in the foreground of this picture. And here, too, is another piece of the ruinous unoccupied space, which . . . runs nearly the whole round of the interior of the shrunken city."

The mosque of Omar with its minaret is at middle left.

Today the Old City of Jerusalem is no more than an appendage of the modern city, and accounts for no more than a tenth or twelfth of the new built-up area. Despite some examples of fine contemporary architecture, the vulgarity and venality of much of the latest building is to be deplored. However, one must also bear in mind what has happened in neighboring Cairo. For example, it has been proposed that the environs of the pyramids of Giza would be improved by the construction of a golf course and by the erection of a brand new pyramid by a consortium of Japanese businessmen. Frank Sinatra has crooned at the base of the Pyramid of Khufu at a special gala attended by the President of Egypt.

62 JERUSALEM: THE MOSQUE OF EL-AQSA

The reverse angle to Plate 60. The Church of the Ascension is on the skyline. The Fountain of the Virgin and the village of Siloam are at the middle right of the picture, in the Valley of Jehoshaphat, and where the path comes curving under the city walls is the Valley of Hinnom. Just out of shot behind the camera are the Tomb of David and the Zion Gate.

When the traveler has entered the Zion Gate and proceeds close by the wall, in the direction of the Temple area, says Frith, "he will probably pass on the outskirts of the Jews' quarter a number of leprous persons of both sexes, who crouch up the way-side—clamorously soliciting alms from the passer. . . . In this outskirt of the city, moreover, not only the eye is offended, but all the senses suffer severely. . . . There is evidently at this point [where his camera stood], some twenty-five feet of rubbish over the original level of the soil; and this is probably not much more than the average deposit which is now spread over the whole city."

The Jewish quarter, with the Christian, Armenian and Muslim quarters, was one of the four original quarters of the ancient city, which was certainly an occupied site as long ago as the fourth millennium B.C. After the Bar-Kokba revolt of 132–135 A.D., the Jews were banished by Hadrian from their own city; their Temple had already been destroyed in 70 A.D. by Titus. They did not become a significant element again until they were brought back to the city as a result of the Egyptian occupation by Mohammed Ali in 1832–1841. By 1900 they had become the single largest community.

The el-Aqsa mosque occupies a prominent place on the sacred area called by the Muslims the Haram es-Sherif. It is situated 600 feet to the south of the Dome of the Rock (see Plate 65). Its name, el-Masjid el-Aqsa, signifies "The Remote Place of Adoration," i.e. remote from Mecca. It was built by the Ommayad Caliph el-Walid I (705–715) and restored after an earthquake by the Abbasid Caliph el-Mahdi, about 780. It was substantially enlarged about 1035 by the Fatimid Caliph az-Zahir, and Saladin and later rulers also made additions. The Crusaders turned it into a Christian *Templum Domini,* and it was used as a headquarters by the Templars, who stabled their horses in its cellars.

63   JERUSALEM: THE CHURCH OF THE HOLY SEPULCHRE

The Church, standing on the traditional site of Golgotha or Calvary, was originally raised by the Emperor Constantine (323–337 A.D.) and his Empress Helena. It was sacked by the Persians under Khosroe II (died 628), rebuilt, and destroyed again by the mad Caliph Hakim, whose insane career and whose mosque in Cairo were described in the commentary to Plate 6. In the reign of his successor it was restored to its former state by the Patriarch Nicephorus and received its main outlines at the hands of the Crusader architects, who enlarged it and consecrated it in 1149. It then survived more or less intact until 1808, when it was gutted by fire.

Frith approved the fidelity with which its Roman and Orthodox curators once again tackled the work of restoration, using the original materials. But he adds: "An observer unused to the East will be astonished at the neglect which is apparent in a building held in higher reverence than any other by the Eastern Christians, and not very long since restored at great cost. There is not only an air of general dilapidation, but on a ledge beneath one of the windows is an unsightly crowd of jars and the like, protected by a rude rail, while a ladder, attached to the wall, forms a means of descending to the ledge. The mosques and churches, except those of the Armenians, and some of the Greeks, almost invariably show the utmost neglect; beautiful portions being walled up, as is the case with the doorway to the right in the present instance, and fragile ornamental details, which a little care would save, being suffered to go to ruin."

64   JERUSALEM: THE POOL OF HEZEKIAH

The Pool of Hezekiah is south of the Church of the Holy Sepulchre, which is at center left of the picture. The buildings on the far side of the Pool are those of the Coptic Monastery and the Greek Monastery, while the motley structures overhanging it on the right are the windows and balconies of the European-run hotels.

We learn from the Second Book of Kings that Hezekiah "made the pool and the conduit and brought water into the city," and from the Second Book of Chronicles that he "stopped the upper watercourse of Gihon and brought it straight down to the west side of the city of David."

The Holy Land appears to have aroused in Frith, with his mid-Victorian piety and close knowledge of the Bible, a somewhat greater degree of enthusiasm and alertness than Egypt and Nubia. The latter regions elicited his interest as an antiquarian and, with their marvelous monuments and the unique quality of their light, offered a wider scope for his skills as a photographer; but the sacred soil of Palestine touched an altogether deeper chord in him which is reflected in the increased liveliness of what he called the "articles" that accompanied his plates. Here, for example, is part of his "article" on the Pool of Hezekiah:

"I cannot write lightly of Holy Palestine. It is true that the natural features of the country are, for the most part, monotonous and comparatively uninteresting—that the towns are paltry and dirty in the extreme—that the Turkish Mohammedan population is ignorant and bigoted—that the Arabs who infest its solitudes are the laziest, the most cowardly, and worthless set of fellows—in a word, and in every sense of it, the greatest vagabonds in existence; yet, in spite of all this, and overwhelming it all triumphantly, comes the thrilling recollection—that this was the country of Abraham and the Prophets! these the cities of David! and—first and last, and mingling with every line of its eventful history—that this was the spot of his earth chosen by its Creator from the beginning, upon which the plan of his salvation should be finished."

65   JERUSALEM: THE POOL OF BETHESDA

A last look at what Frith, in a felicitous phrase, called "this fallen queen of cities." The picture is taken from a point inside the city wall near the blocked-in archways of St. Stephen's Gate, which is visible in the right-hand stretch of wall in Plate 60. The Mosque of Omar is at the upper left, and the huddled houses of the Turkish and Arab city are at the upper right.

The photograph gives a clear impression of the appearance of the Haram es-Sherif, the platform-like area of the Mohammedan sanctuary, in the middle of the last century. The Mosque of Omar, the Kubt es-Lukkra or Dome of the Rock, was founded on Mount Moriah by the Caliph Omar I, who took possession of Jerusalem in 638. Omar's mosque vanished, and the present mosque was actually built by the Caliph Abd el-Malik and completed in 691, to mark the fact that Jerusalem had been visited by Mohammed and ranked as the third most honored shrine after Mecca and Medina. It was Suleiman the Magnificent who, in 1552, added the blue-and-green external tiles, in imitation of the mosques of Turkey and Persia.

In the Haram es-Sherif, in 1099, the Crusaders under Godfrey of Bouillon, who was later to be interred in the Church of the Holy Sepulchre, slaughtered 10,000 (Christian version) or 70,000 (Muslim version) men, women and children. The entire precinct ran ankle deep in blood. The Church erected by the Crusaders on the site was dismantled in 1187 by the conquering Saladin, who put an end to the Christian kingdom of Jerusalem that had existed between 1099 and 1187. Saladin purified the spot with jars of rose water brought from Damascus.

The Christians briefly regained the city between 1229 and 1239, and again in 1243–1244. In 1247 Jerusalem became a fief of the Egyptian Mamelukes, who ruled until the Ottoman ruler Selim I took it in 1517, establishing the Turkish dominion that was to last until the British entered Jerusalem under Field-Marshal Lord Allenby in 1917.

66 HEBRON

Hebron, 17 miles south of Jerusalem, is a town which for most of its existence has been fortunate enough to live in relative peace and security. Scarcely mentioned in the Old Testament, and not at all in the New, it was nonetheless the city where David was anointed king over all Israel, where he ruled for seven years, and where Absalom raised the standard of revolt. It was briefly a bishopric in Crusading days (1100–1187) before passing into Mohammedan hands.

Its tranquility was rudely shattered in 1834, when its citizens were foolish enough to offer resistance to Ibrahim Pasha, the son of Mohammed Ali (see commentaries to Plates 4 and 5). Ibrahim Pasha was a first-rate soldier who in the previous ten years had conquered what is now Saudi Arabia, had established Egyptian rule in the Sudan, had intervened in Greece, and was now marching victoriously through Palestine and Syria toward Constantinople with every sign of succeeding in his aim of overthrowing the Ottoman Empire—an aim which it took the combined efforts of Britain, France and Russia to thwart. Ibrahim sacked and pillaged Hebron and put its inhabitants to the sword.

Frith's picture demonstrates that the city seems to have made an excellent recovery from the stirring events of a quarter of a century earlier. At that time it was a sleepy and dignified little town with a mainly Jewish population of 10,000. The Jews left Hebron almost totally in 1929, following a series of Arab riots, and did not return in force until after the 1967 war. Still technically belonging to the Jordanian West Bank, the Arab quarter is now totally dwarfed by the continuous Jewish high-rises on the slopes of Mount Hebron.

Abraham, Isaac and Jacob passed much of their lives in the vicinity of Hebron, and were reputedly buried there, together with Rebecca, Sarah and Leah, in a cave that now lies beneath the principal mosque. It was from Hebron that Abraham set out for the land of Egypt.

67 THE MONASTERY OF SAN SABA

A masterly study of the monastery at which Frith made a halt in the Valley of Kidron, on his way north to Jericho and the Dead Sea. A "magnificently wide and deep ravine forms a sternly appropriate clinging-place for this old ascetic pile."

The monastery was founded between 478 and 491 by St. Sabas, a cantankerous old hermit from Cappadocia. When well over 70, he sallied forth with his monks and joined his fellow abbots in ousting the representatives of the Monophysite faction from Jerusalem. He evidently throve on combat and controversy, for he died at the age of 94 in 532.

The complicated religious squabbles and heresies of Christian Pales-tine resulted in a series of miniature civil wars in which one set of monks would alternately drive another from its monastery; but at San Saba the buildings at least survived, and its Greek Orthodox occupants made a living out of providing food and shelter for pilgrims and caravans.

Frith's photograph shows numerous caves in the cliffs above the monastery. These, says Frith, are "cell-like apertures, some of them partly built up with masonry: these were once the abodes of ascetics, who had devoted themselves for the remainder of life to this dismal entombment, depending even for their daily food upon the monks of the convent."

68 THE NORTH SHORE OF THE DEAD SEA

After Jerusalem, the Dead Sea was at the head of the Victorian travelers' itinerary in the Palestine area. Often they would have themselves photographed in their voluminous "bathing costumes," floating on its brackish waves with a book in one hand and a parasol in the other.

Frith spared us that. Instead, on a day in May in which he tells us that the temperature was 130 degrees, he composed this haunting study.

The Arabic name for the Dead Sea, which is fed by the River Jordan and is 1292 feet below sea level, is the Bahr el-Lut, or Sea of Lot. Fifty miles away, on its southern margin, stand Sodom and its four sister cities, including Gomorrah, which were overwhelmed when the salt sea rose and burst its banks.

69 NABLUS

Like Hebron, the town of Nablus, 35 miles due north of Jerusalem, was a part of Palestine under the terms of the British Mandate of 1922, was allotted to Transjordan as a result of the U.N. Partition Plan of 1947, and passed into Israeli hands after the 1967 war. It possesses the largest Arab population of any of the West Bank towns; in 1976 its population was estimated as 42,000.

The ancient Sichem or Schechem, on the slopes of Mount Ebal, was one of the towns of the Levites. It was the capital of the kingdoms of Abimelech and Jeroboam and the chief seat of the Samaritans. It was destroyed by John Hyrcanus I in 129 B.C., but was rebuilt by the Emperor Hadrian and named Neapolis, from which its present name derives. It was the place where Abraham sojourned and where Jacob bought a tract of land which he gave to Joseph. Frith was pleased with the "white town, embosomed in . . . verdure," and considered that it was "a pleasing proof of the good taste and sound judgment of those venerable patriarchs in matters residential and agricultural." He added: "It is now a thriving town of some 10,000 or 12,000 inhabitants, with extensive manufactories of soap and other articles."

70 NAZARETH

Nazareth is 67 miles north of Jerusalem and 35 from Nablus. Like Nablus, it had been an important prehistoric site, but is not mentioned in the Old Testament. It became the village which was the home of Jesus, and subsequently had a tragic history as it constantly changed hands between Arabs, Christians and Jews.

Frith quotes an "expression of an old topographer," which is "as happy as it is poetical:—Nazareth is a rose, and like a rose has the same rounded form, enclosed by mountains as the flower by its leaves."

Now the district capital of Galilee, in 1976 it had a population of 26,500.

71 TIBERIAS

Tiberias, on Lake Tiberias or the Sea of Galilee, was the center of Roman military activity in the northern portion of its province of Palestine. The Romans chose it because it was midway between Damascus and Caesarea, and also because it possessed therapeutic mineral springs. Its most ancient buildings dated from the time of the Tetrarch Herod Antipas, who named the town in honor of the Emperor Tiberius (14–37 A.D.). It remained a military outpost until the Middle Ages, and was fortified by both Arabs and Crusaders. After the destruction of Jerusalem it became an important center of Jewish learning.

Today it has a population of over 20,000, but in Frith's time it had only 3000 inhabitants and still showed the effects of a devastating earthquake in 1837. Apart from the striking character of the Roman remains, Frith declared that the town itself was "a most wretchedly forlorn and dirty-looking assemblage of houses, or hovels of ultra-oriental character. . . . There is an adage, 'that the king of the fleas holds his court in Tiberias.' This we had vividly in mind on our arrival at the spot, and so were steeled against the strong inclination of our Bedouins to pitch our tents within the walls. Escaping this infliction, we arranged that the clear blue waters of the hallowed lake should almost wash the threshold of our tents . . . . We enjoyed a most refreshing bathe; and . . . could see multitudes of fine fish in the bright water below. . . . It will be remembered that here was the scene of the miraculous draught of fishes: yet there is now only one crazy old boat on the lake!"

72 GAZA

Gaza has always had the dubious privilege of lying directly on the line of march of the innumerable armies tramping out of or into the land of Egypt. A garrison town of the Egyptian Empire, it later became one of the five main cities of Philistia. Plutarch has described vividly how Alexander the Great conducted in person one of its many protracted sieges, and was wounded during the course of operations. It was at Gaza that Demetrius I Poliorcetes of Macedonia was defeated by Alexander's satrap Ptolemy I Soter in 312 B.C. The most famous episode in its annals was the captivity and humiliation of the blinded Samson and his destruction of the house of Dagon. Subsequently it fell under the sway of the monarchies of Israel and Judah.

Although it was routinely besieged by the Crusaders, it was permitted to molder more or less unmolested through the remainder of the Middle Ages, and only experienced something of a revival during the last decades of the nineteenth century and the early decades of the twentieth. Frith found it an agreeable but completely undistinguished city, pleasantly decked out with palm trees, and he quoted the famous line from *Samson Agonistes:* "Gaza yet stands, but all her sons are fallen."

Part of Palestine under the British Mandate, Gaza became Egyptian after the Armistice Demarcation Line was drawn in 1949, and was annexed by the Israelis together with the remainder of the so-called Gaza Strip in 1967. The Gaza Strip is currently a no-man's-land, crowded with almost three-quarters of a million Arab refugees who exist either in makeshift camps or in somewhat more permanent residences. The city of Gaza alone now has a population that has swollen to at least 250,000 people.

73 BAALBEK: THE GREAT PILLARS

Thirty-five miles northwest of Damascus, Baalbek, in modern Lebanon, was the most northerly point reached by Frith on his Near Eastern travels. The famous monument had been many times described and delineated by other European visitors, from the account which was written in 1507 by Martin von Baumgarten onward. On the other hand, its precise character and attributions remained obscure to them and to Frith himself, who in the accompanying "articles" to his three photographs of the temple nowhere offers any guess as to its origins. The isolation, the mystery and the grandeur of Baalbek were quite sufficient and satisfying for the Victorian traveler.

Baalbek, the ancient Heliopolis, or City of the Sun, consists of two Roman temples with their appendages, built on a site that was already ancient when the Romans, in the time of Augustus, established it as a *colonia* for the pensioned veterans of two of the legions. The larger of the two temples, which took two centuries to build and was completed in the third century A.D., is dedicated to Jupiter Heliopolitanus; the smaller one, built about 150 A.D. and attached to the southern wall of the courtyard of the larger one, is dedicated to Bacchus. It is fitting that a temple to Jupiter, in his avatar as successor to Baal or Bel, the ancient Phoenician sun god, should have been erected in such brilliant, sun-saturated surroundings. Both temples are visible in the photograph.

A French traveler in the sixteenth century claims to have seen 27 columns of the greater temple in place; a century later the number was reported as nine; and the reliable and indefatigable Englishman Richard Pococke states that in 1743, as now, only six columns were standing. The six slender columns that remain are over 60 feet tall, and originally there were no less than 54, surrounding the statue of the god. The columns consisted of three expertly articulated sections strengthened by means of an internal iron rod. It was for the sake of the iron that Arab nomads later broke up the pillars that had fallen.

74   BAALBEK: SMALL TEMPLE

This is not the temple of Bacchus, but a little octagonal temple a few yards in front of the portico of the temple of Jupiter. At one time it had been converted into a Greek Orthodox chapel. Like the twin temples of which it is an adjunct, it was cracked and damaged by the great earthquake of 1170 A.D. Frith writes: "This exquisitely beautiful little temple . . . stands almost within the modern village, some of the walls of which are seen in the foreground of my picture."

Baalbek today has a population of 16,000. Until the onset of the tragic Lebanese civil war it was the site of an imaginative and well-attended summer festival of theater, music and opera.

It is interesting to reflect that, only a dozen years before Frith made his peculiarly modern photographic studies of Baalbek, one of the last of the line of great Romantic painter-topographers, David Roberts, was sketching the site for inclusion in his *The Holy Land, Syria, Idumea, Arabia, Egypt & Nubia*. Thus do artistic and technical epochs intermingle and overlap.

75 DAMASCUS

Frith was dissatisfied with this panoramic study of what the Victorians believed was "the oldest city in the world." We must acknowledge, he says, "that the camera does very scanty justice—we might almost say does an injustice—to subjects so distant, and so minute and indistinct in their details as this is; but had we not attempted it (though on a very rough, unfavourable day), we should, in all probability, have suffered the heavy displeasure of the critics who have read of such a scene, or possibly have even beheld it."

Damascus—which is certainly very old, and was a city even before 2000 B.C., the time of Abraham—did not impress Frith. We have seen that he did not appear happy when brought into close contact with the Arab of his day. We have quoted earlier instances of his distaste for Arab towns and Arab customs. He particularly appeared to resent Arab overcharging and incessant demands for *baksheesh*. The Victorians, after all, had a censorious and puritanical attitude toward begging and the spectacle of poverty.

"The population of Damascus," he concludes, "is probably upwards of 150,000 souls [1977: upwards of a million]. Silk fabrics, some of them richly interwoven with silver, are still made here; few travellers escape from Damascus without having bartered sundry pieces of good useful gold for huge, flaring, long-tasseled silk handkerchiefs to wrap about their heads, and preposterous scarfs, many yards long, to wind round and round their already overheated persons. The manufacture of swords and gun-barrels, for which Damascus was for centuries so justly celebrated, has now degenerated into a state of art which would shock a Birmingham maker of seven-and-sixpenny muskets."

76 DAMASCUS: INSIDE THE CITY

A view over the old city, with the Great or Omayyad Mosque, largely the work of the Caliphs el-Walid and Omar II, at left rear. In the background are the mountains of the Anti-Lebanon.

"Damascus, then, upon the whole, disappointed my somewhat extravagant expectations. I had imagined a forest of minarets, as in Cairo and Constantinople, but my view displays almost the only mosque in the city. The splendid mansions of the luxurious Damascus, overlaid with mosaics, and sparkling with fountains, resolve themselves into the rickety fabrics revealed in the Photograph, mysteriously tacked together with scraps of lath and timber, and plastered with that hot yellow mud. It is true that the interior courts of some of these wretched-looking tenements are fantastically brilliant and splendid; the mosaics are there; the tinsel and the fountains are there: but be satisfied, O European luxuriast, to admire and enjoy them at a distance. Peep in; just catch the *coup d'oeil*, and retire: or, if determined to linger, throw thyself in dreamy blissfulness upon a divan, and listen to the tinkling of the fountain, and gaze with half-closed eyes at the opposite side of the court. Scrutinize not too closely the painting of that balcony; fret not thyself in any wise about the jointing of the marble pavement; attempt not, I beseech thee, to square those door-panels or window-frames with the straight-edge of thine eye (in the East there are no straight lines, no squares, no circles); the shade is welcome, the green of the orange and rose trees is refreshing; blue and gold are beautiful colours; believe, smoke, and be happy!"

77   DAMASCUS: THE STREET CALLED STRAIGHT

A last, characteristic, evocative study: the street where St. Paul (died 67 A.D.) is traditionally held to have lodged after his conversion, framed by the Roman-built Bab es-Shurki or East Gate. The Biblical reference is in Acts 9:11. "The Street Called Straight" is probably that part of the Suk el-Tawileh ("the Long Bazaar") which is still called the Darb el-Mustakim ("Straight Street").

We may close with Frith's own *envoi*:

"The demand for the work was from the first, and still continues to be, much greater than can be supplied, owing to the slowness of the process of photographic 'printing.' Some of my readers are, perhaps, not aware that the original pictures were taken on glass, and that from these, as from a copper-plate, each single impression is taken by an expensive and tedious photographic process. More than 2000 copies have already been taken from each of the 'negatives' of this series, and the originals are still as perfect as ever. I flatter myself that the style of printing which has been employed is very superior in brilliancy and 'tone,' and time alone will decide whether it is, as I believe it to be, permanent. Trusting that my readers will continue to extend the kind indulgence to my spirited Publisher which the difficulty and novelty of his efforts deserve, and again thanking them heartily for their generous approbation, I make, most respectfully, MY SALAAM!"